Allergy-Free Cooking

How to Avoid the Eight Major Food
Allergens and Eat Happily Ever After

By Eileen Rhude Yoder, Ph.D.

Milk, Egg, Wheat, Soy, Peanut,
Tree Nuts, Fish, and Shellfish

RUNNING PRESS
PHILADELPHIA · LONDON

Cover Photo Credits:
Milk: ©Ted Morrison/FoodPix/Jupiterimages
Shrimp: ©Nicholas Eveleigh/Iconica/Getty Images
Nuts: ©Brian Hagiwara/Brand X Pictures/Jupiterimages
Eggs: ©Lew Robertson/FoodPix/Jupiterimages
Peanuts: ©Lars Klove/Stone/Getty Images
Edamame: ©Jonathan Kantor/The Image Bank/Getty Images
Salmon: ©Jeff Oshiro/FoodPix/Jupiterimages
Wheat: ©Michael Rosenfeld/Photographer's Choice/Getty Images

Portions of chapter 5 are adapted from "Maintaining Patient Compliance During an Elimination Diet," by E. Yoder from *Handbook of Food Allergy*, edited by James C. Breneman, Vol. 29, pp. 239–246 of the Immunology Series, © 1987 by Marcel-Dekker, Inc., New York, and reprinted with their kind permission.

9 8 7 6 5 4 3 2

Digit on the right indicates the number of this printing

Library of Congress Control Number:
ISBN: 978-0-7624-3349-0

Book design by Amanda Richmond
Edited by Geoffrey Stone
Typography: Lomba & Abadi

Running Press Book Publishers
2300 Chestnut Street
Philadelphia, Pennsylvania 19103-4371

Visit us on the web!
www.runningpresscooks.com

In memory of my father, Howard,
and my brother, Dennis.
I miss you both so much.

And to our future generation:
Brent, Jordan, Joshua,
Stephen, Erin, Eliana, and Alexis

Contents

Foreword 6

Preface to the First Edition 8

Preface to the Second Edition 11

Acknowledgments 13

PART ONE: PLANNING

1. Beginning an Allergy-Free Diet 15

2. Getting Organized 25

3. Identifying Allergens 37

4. Allergy-Free Shopping 55

5. Cooking Suggestions and Substitutions 72

6. Children and Food Allergies 85

PART TWO: RECIPES

7. Meal Planning and Menus 99

8. Beverages 111

9. Breads, Muffins, Biscuits, and Crackers 124

10. Cereals and Pancakes 147

11. Salads and Salad Dressings 158

12. Soups and Stews 187

13. Vegetables and Side Dishes 203

14. Main Courses 224

15. Cookies, Bars, Fruit Treats, and Snacks 241

16. Cakes, Pies, and Puddings 272

17. Staples, Condiments, Sauces, and Spreads 299

Appendix 315

Index 330

Foreword

I have spent the past thirty years of my professional life treating people with food allergies. The technical and scientific elements of diagnosis and treatment have advanced amazingly in recent years. However, the down-to-earth question of how and what to feed these patients has always been a problem. It has become even more difficult with the tremendous additions to our food supply. Instead of forty to fifty simple foods, our dietary intake now includes a possible 7,000 different foodstuffs, additives, chemicals, and drugs. Little wonder that the allergy diet poses a big problem for the preparer.

This book sets out to simplify and clarify. Dr. Yoder has spent many years studying the faults of available foods and diets, looking for suppliers of pure foods and ingredients, and experimenting with food preparation. She shows clearly that one is able to provide a tasty, nutritious, yet safe diet for the allergic patient.

This product of Dr. Yoder's many years of study and work is a marvelous addition to the physician's tools. The difficult part—providing a diet for diagnosis and for treatment—can be handled expeditiously with this book. If a patient (or parent) can read, he or she should be able to maintain allergy-free nutrition without sacrificing the joy of eating. In fact, Dr. Yoder describes meal preparation in such detail that it sounds as though even I, a kitchen klutz, could do it—and have fun.

Allergy-Free Cooking is easy to use because it is well organized. The completeness of the presentation is represented by the thirty recipes in the chapter on cookies, each sounding very original and delicious. Dr. Yoder has even found intriguing uses for bananas.

Dr. Yoder has also given very practical methods for coping with traveling, holidays, and parties, all of which can be trying for the allergic patient. Various chapters describe shopping, substitutions, and precautions. Parents will find these eye-opening ideas a godsend.

I have always maintained that the allergic patient does not have to starve to death or be bored to death on an allergy diet. This book is readable proof of my conviction. I plan to use it extensively.

Allergy-Free Cooking comes at a most opportune time. Estimates suggest that over half of the U.S. population has ingestant problems, many allergic. This book will provide essential information to a great number of patients who probably have been waiting for such a practical book.

J. C. Breneman, M.D., A.B.A.I.
Four-time Chairman
International Food Allergy Symposium

Preface to the
First Edition

My daughters, Laura and Patty, who are now teenagers, were sick from the day they were born. I took them from doctor to doctor. Finally, they were diagnosed as having severe allergies. And I also discovered I had just as many food allergies as they had!

It was a long time before we finally regained our health. The girls were sick much of the time and needed close medical supervision. However, we all learned to adjust our diets and not let food allergies limit our lifestyles. In fact, because of their allergies, I have encouraged the girls to be as active as possible. They are both adventurers; Laura has been camping and horseback riding in the Rocky Mountains, white-water rafting and mountain climbing in Idaho, jet skiing and wind surfing in Florida, and hang gliding in Tennessee! Patty is just as active, camping and traveling around the country, water and snow skiing, and participating on her school track and softball teams.

At first, however, it wasn't easy to adjust to having food allergies. I was discouraged with the bland and boring meals we were eating. I read every cookbook on food allergies available, but all I found were recipes that eliminated a few allergens such as milk, eggs, and wheat. At the time there weren't many books for people sensitive to other foods. So I went to different health food stores and bought interesting and unusual foods to add some flavor to our diets. I began to experiment with different ingredients and create new recipes. The results were terrific. I realized that despite our food allergies, we could still have delicious and exciting meals.

Along with my appetite for experimenting in the kitchen, I hungered for more information to help us understand and cope with our food allergies.

Being a nurse at the time, I went to the medical libraries and read everything I could on allergies. Slowly but surely I was gratified to see the study of food allergies emerge as a new medical science. This persuaded me to get my Ph.D. in nutrition.

Soon I found local doctors requesting that I see their patients and counsel them on meal management of food allergies. After answering the same questions a few hundred times, I decided to create a booklet with a few recipes and tips on living with food allergies.

I set up a research kitchen, hired a staff, and began to develop hypoallergenic recipes. With more time and practice, I grew increasingly satisfied with the quality of the recipes and was able to create more interesting concoctions.

In my "spare" time I began traveling all over North America, lecturing about food allergies and appearing on various television and radio shows. I received so much mail from people who wanted to share a recipe or offer practical advice on how they managed their diet, I decided to publish a newsletter entitled *Food Allergy and Nutrition Newsletter.*

I received many requests from readers who needed help with their specific food allergies. Using this feedback, I began research on a computer-generated allergy-free diet that would offer recipes and cooking information tailor-made to the person's individual requirements. It took three years of intense work to develop the program. The end result is an extensive notebook similar to the one you will learn to create in chapter 2.

This book incorporates the information and research developed for the computerized diet, the recipes I have developed over the years for my family and in our research kitchen, and the excellent advice I have received from readers and allergists all over the country. My hope is that it will help you get started on your way to a healthier and happier life. If you have any questions or comments, or would like information about attending a workshop or having me conduct one in your area, write to me and I'll do my best to respond quickly.

Eileen Rhude Yoder, Ph.D.
1987

Preface to the Second Edition

I can't believe that my book has been in print now for almost a quarter of a century. Thank you, readers. In that time, my children have grown to adults. Laura is a pilot for a major airline and still has fixed allergies, especially to soy. She has to pack her meals and carry them with her for her four- to six-day flights. Patty is a mom and has outgrown most of her allergies, but now my grandson has allergies. My niece, Jamie, had numerous allergies as a child and now her daughter, Erin, has allergies to fish. My mother still has food allergies. Allergies tend to be inherited, and in my family there are five generations of known food allergies.

Over the last twenty-five years, there have been some advances in testing of food allergies, as well as improvements in the food-labeling laws. These have been a long time coming.

I hope this book helps you when you begin your allergy-free diet. I've had to go through everything I've written about in this book because I have numerous, severe allergies. So I write from first-hand experience. And I know the awful feeling of having a severe asthma attack and no air moving in my lungs. I also experienced such a severe anaphylactic reaction that I spent three weeks in the hospital and then years of relearning due to brain damage from lack of oxygen. I've seen my children suffer every day when they were little. I've been there. I also hope that my experience working with food-allergic patients will help you understand your allergies better.

If you will help me, I plan on writing a book that will have a multitude of recipes shared by you. If you have any recipes or tips, or stories you would like to share, please send them in. It helps everyone with food allergies since many people without allergies still don't understand how a smell or small taste can make an allergic person sick.

If you have any questions for me, please contact me at EileenR Yoder@aol.com. On the subject line write URGENT: AFC READER. This will distinguish you from any unwanted ads. I promise to acknowledge you as soon as possible.

Eileen R. Yoder
June 14, 2008

Acknowledgments

I would like to thank Hazel Douglas for her hard work as she retyped my entire book, offered innumerable suggestions, and helped me as we prepared the new book. She also is a great cook and helped test the recipes for the book.

I would also like to thank my mother, Diana Rhude, and Melgrace Omg for proofreading my manuscript.

Part One

PLANNING

1.

Beginning an Allergy-Free Diet

Have you recently been told by your doctor that you or a family member might have food allergies? Has your doctor recommended that you avoid certain foods for a period of time? Or have you noticed that every time you eat a certain food you feel uncomfortable or even ill? Perhaps you have not identified a particular food that causes problems, but you feel that something you eat causes problems.

If so, this book will help you. An allergy-free diet consists of two steps: first, the diagnosis or identification of your specific food allergies and second, the maintenance of your allergy-free diet.

To identify the food or foods you are allergic to, you need to begin an avoidance diet. (This is commonly referred to as the elimination diet and simply means eliminating the allergenic foods.) This diet will enable you to identify the food or foods to which you are allergic by avoiding specific foods that are very often the causes of allergic reactions.

Once you know what your food allergies are, you can then tailor your diet to your specific allergy.

THE AVOIDANCE DIET

To find out if you are allergic to some of the most common foods, the avoidance diet is an important diagnostic tool. If you suspect that you have food allergies, the first step is to visit your physician. Discuss the avoidance or elimination diet recommended in this book with your doctor and use his guidelines in conjunction with the instructions here. In addition to food allergy testing, he may want you to avoid other foods in addition to the allergenic foods eliminated in this book.

Based on the new Food Allergy Labeling and Consumer Protection Act of 2004 (FALCPA) that has been in effect since the beginning of 2006, food manufacturers have to clearly identify their product if it contains any of the eight major food allergens listed under this law. These eight major foods or food groups tend to cause 90% of most allergic reactions in the United States.

Under FALCPA, the law identifies these eight major foods or food groups as *milk, egg, wheat, soybean, peanut, tree nuts, fish*, and *shellfish*. All of the recipes in this book exclude most or all of the major eight allergens in each recipe.

In addition, other common allergens are excluded, including corn and citrus (in the majority of recipes), pepper (including paprika, chilies, and chili pepper), garlic, onion, cinnamon, and coffee, plus additives, preservatives, and coloring.

If you are a tea drinker instead of a coffee drinker, you need to eliminate tea for the period of time you are testing for food allergies. Please don't omit this part of the test, as it could cause a major food sensitivity or food allergy.

I HAD ONE PATIENT, "Susie," who had very severe food reactions. She had been on very high doses of prednisone because of her uncontrolled asthma and undiagnosed food allergies. Because of the prednisone, the doctor couldn't test her for food allergies. So Susie kept a very detailed food diary with her symptoms. Week after week she came in and foods were removed from her diet that caused her problems. She slowly improved but never felt perfect. I thought she was unknowingly not putting everything on her food diary. This happens with most patients but not Susie. She was an office administrator at a large hospital and so her food diary was perfect. She also kept to her diet unwaveringly. I knew she wanted to get better.

Instead of going over her food diary, I began asking her what she did from the moment she got out of bed. I asked her over and over. Finally, she told me that when she got to the office she would have a cup of tea! She thought of it as harmless and never wrote it down. After she eliminated her tea, her whole life turned around. She no longer had asthma attacks, her arthritic reactions went away, and she did not take the prednisone anymore. Now, this took a long time to diagnose her allergies and a lot of work on Susie's part to keep on a very strict diet 100 percent of the time. The point of my story is that even a simple cup of tea or shake of pepper can throw your testing or diagnosis stage off.

Based on my research I have found that the above foods and seasonings cause frequent reactions. Why, you ask? It's because you eat these foods and seasonings almost every day! I don't know of anyone who doesn't automatically add salt and pepper to food. Then most dinners in America start with onion and garlic. Cinnamon is the second most used spice after pepper; it's automatically found in every baked good. Next, most adults must start their day off with a cup of coffee or tea. Corn is found in every food product in America since it can be created into so many forms like high fructose corn syrup, corn oil, etc. Citrus is another food that is eaten or drunk on a daily basis. This repeated exposure, day after day, never allows your body a chance to clear its system of the allergen. My research for this was based on skin test results, blood tests, and food diaries of thousands of clients.

To diagnose your particular food allergies, I recommend that you avoid all of these foods. (This is not as hard as you think; once you have sampled some of the recipes for the avoidance diet in part 2, you may not even miss these foods.)

If your symptoms decrease or disappear by eliminating all of these foods, you are on the right track, and you can introduce foods back to your diet one at a time to determine which ones cause your symptoms. If eliminating all these foods produces no change in your allergies, then you must do some further detective work, so test additional foods such as spices, yeast, beef, and pork. Discuss this with your physician. Begin your diet by getting your physician's approval.

A note about antihistamines: it's also a good idea to ask for guidelines regarding medications because antihistamines may lesson or mask reactions. Also, some doctors require you to stop taking antihistamines three days before skin testing; others do not.

Next, read chapters 1 through 6 to learn how to make the task of beginning and staying on the avoidance diet easier. You'll find helpful information on getting organized, shopping for groceries, and cooking.

Browse through the recipes in part 2 and pick out a few you want to try. Also look at the sample menus on pages 102–107 to get some ideas for meals you and your family will enjoy. (It is a good idea if the entire family stays on this diet. It saves time in meal preparation and keeps the person on the allergy-free diet from being tempted to eat the foods he's trying to avoid.)

Stay on the avoidance diet for at least one week or more until you are symptom free, unless your doctor recommends otherwise, because allergens can remain in the body up to five days.

SETBACKS

While on the diet, it is extremely important to remember that even ingesting a slight amount of the allergenic food can produce symptoms, so you must not deviate from the diet, thinking that it won't hurt to have just a taste. If by chance you accidentally eat an allergenic food, continue with the diet. This happens quite often with all the confusion in changing to an all new diet. Sometimes you overlook an ingredient. You must now spend two hours each time you go grocery shopping just reading labels. I still read all the food labels, every time I go grocery shopping, because the food manufacturers change ingredients without warning. Occasionally I still accidentally buy foods that cause an allergic reaction.

Stay on the diet for another week from the date of the ingestion of the suspected allergenic food. *Don't become discouraged* since this happens to almost everyone, especially children! I tell everyone, if you imagine you are trying to put out a fire (the allergic reaction), you can't keep feeding it wood (food) to burn.

If at all possible, avoid all contact with these allergens. Just inhaling the odors of some foods can cause allergic symptoms in very sensitive people. Write up your menus, buy your groceries, and cook some foods first. You can't stay on a diet if you don't have foods available. If possible, pack away or give away the foods you can't eat.

CRAVINGS

Most likely, you will have terrible cravings for the foods you are most allergic to and might go through withdrawal. Since I have so many food allergies, I rotate many of my foods. Some foods I eat once every four days; other foods I eat twice a month. Of all the foods that I must limit, sugar and wheat cause severe cravings. Sometimes, I find that I slowly start to eat a little more sugar or wheat each week until that's all I can think of to eat. I've gone over my tolerance level and start to have symptoms. Then I have to go through a terrible withdrawal when I have to give up those foods for a month or more. For me, it's truly awful. It takes two weeks for my system to be cleared. I get terrible headaches and all my joints hurt. I'm telling you this so you might get a better understanding of some reactions.

Not all foods will cause a craving, but it's pretty common the first time you start eliminating foods since you're eliminating a multitude of foods. Of course it's nothing like a drug or cigarette withdrawal.

ONE DAY, THE MOTHER OF one of my patients came in crying. She told me her eight year old son had been arrested for stealing. I listened to her empathetically until she told me that it was a slice of American cheese that he'd stolen! Then I laughed, and told her not to worry, her son was going through withdrawal from milk. I again explained to her what might happen during withdrawal from a food. I wrote a note for the judge and the young boy was soon eating goat's cheese at home.

TESTING FOODS

Once your allergy symptoms disappear, you can add foods back to your diet, one at a time, to see which ones produce reactions. You must test each of the foods you have been avoiding on the diet. To test a food, for instance corn, eliminate corn in all forms for one week. Then eat generous portions of pure corn, such as pure corn syrup, corn on the cob, or unsugared corn flakes, for three consecutive days. On the first day, eat a small amount (such as two tablespoons of canned corn) then eat a regular size portion (half a cup) at the next meal.

If allergic symptoms develop, stop eating the corn. If allergic symptoms do not develop after eating pure corn products for three days, you can probably assume that corn is acceptable. Do not eat corn while you test the next food in the same manner. *Wait three days before you test the next food* since you may have a delayed reaction to corn.

If symptoms reappear, you'll have to avoid the food for several more months, then retest once more. If nothing happens, you can add the food back into your diet. Your doctor should guide you through this testing phase.

THE MAINTENANCE DIET

Once you know what your specific food allergies are, you can begin a maintenance diet. This is a diet specially tailored to your food allergies. You can use the recipes in part 2 of this book, adding back those ingredients to which you are not allergic.

Once you begin the maintenance diet, continue filling out your food diary (see pages 29–31) and other records in your notebook as explained in chapter 2. It's important to continue maintaining your food diary after you have determined your food allergies because you might discover new allergies to the new ingredients that you've never eaten before or to foods eaten less frequently. For example, my major food allergies were diagnosed through testing, so I cooked with my new "allergy-free" ingredients. I soon noticed that I kept developing a migraine when I made certain baked goods. It took me a short while to figure out it was the cinnamon, not the new ingredients. To double check, I simply mixed sugar and cinnamon and sprinkled it on my oatmeal bread. No doubt about it, I developed an instant migraine headache.

IMMEDIATE AND DELAYED REACTIONS

That type of reaction to cinnamon that I just described is called an immediate reaction. It usually occurs immediately after a food is ingested. Immediate reactions can have an explosive onset within minutes or can be delayed up to two hours after ingesting the offending food. The most notable immediate reaction is anaphylactic shock, where symptoms can range from spontaneous remission to death within minutes. I developed severe anaphylactic shock and ended up in the hospital for three weeks after I accidentally came into contact with some unknown dental material. If you or your child have these severe food reactions, your doctor will give you special medications including an EpiPen or EpiPen, Jr. See *www.epipen.com.*

You should also wear a Medic-Alert bracelet; see *www.medic-alert.org.*

In cases of immediate reactions, the cause of the food allergy is often obvious because of the quick reaction. Some people even develop an instinctive avoidance or dislike for the taste or even smell of the offending food. So, if your child tends to have food allergies, listen to him when he says he hates a food. Children usually develop immediate reactions, whereas adults usually develop *delayed reactions* (occurring from two hours to five days later).

In some cases, these immediate reactions can be *permanent or fixed.* Permanent allergies to certain foods are less likely to be outgrown; among those are peanuts, nuts, and shellfish.

Most food-allergic children, however, tend to outgrow allergies to certain foods such as milk, eggs, wheat, and soy. This isn't 100 percent though, as my grown daughter has a fixed allergy to soy.

DELAYED REACTIONS

Delayed reactions are the most common reactions in adults. They are the most difficult to diagnose because they cause *chronic, constant* symptoms. For example, you may complain of such vague symptoms as a chronic headache, fatigue, irritability, pains in muscles and joints. These symptoms never go away, so you can't easily diagnose your food allergies unless you have tests and/or keep a food diary.

Now that you have a better understanding about how to start your allergy-free diet, read the next five chapters. Then write up a personalized plan of how you want to start and maintain your diet.

2.

Getting Organized

Keeping a careful record of your symptoms can often be the key to success on an allergy-free diet. In fact, a notebook with pertinent information on your particular food allergies can be an invaluable tool. For this purpose I recommend buying a hardcover three-ring binder with dividers with pockets. Keep a separate notebook for each family member who has food allergies.

Your notebook should include the topics listed below, which I will describe separately.

1. Food diary
2. Foods to avoid
3. List of allowed foods, grocery list, and food sources
4. Menus
5. Cooking suggestions and substitutions
6. Recipe development
7. Recipes
8. Miscellaneous

KEEPING A FOOD DIARY

In order to identify the foods that cause you to have allergic reactions, you will find that an accurate record of the foods you eat and your symptoms is indispensable. Keeping a food diary is simple as long as you remind yourself to do it. Just follow these three steps:

1. Make copies of the food diary on page 29. Be sure to date and number the pages. Always carry the current day's diet sheet with you and immediately record the foods eaten.
2. Write down everything you eat or drink, including the date and time. List all the ingredients of mixed foods. For example, a chicken salad sandwich might be listed as whole wheat bread, butter, mayonnaise, celery, pepper, and chicken.
3. List all of your symptoms, indicating the degree of severity, when the symptoms occurred, and how long the reaction lasted. You may wish to use a scale of 1 to 10 to indicate the degree of a reaction, with 1 being a very mild reaction and 10 being the worst type of reaction. For young children, you might get them to draw faces of how they feel.

SAMPLE FOOD DIARY

Date: 04/01/09

TIME OF MEAL	FOOD/DRINK/ MEDICINE	TIME OF SYMPTOMS	SYMPTOMS
7:00 AM	Tea, rice cereal, milk	9:00 AM	Headache (5) 20 min.
10:00 AM	Apple	12:45 PM	No symptom
12:30 PM	Chicken salad sandwich (bread, butter, mayon- naise chicken, pepper, celery), milk	1:45 PM	Hives on face (5) 30 min. Headache (9) 2 hours
5:30 PM	Steak, baked potato, sour cream, corn, milk	7:00 PM	Headache (9) 2 hours

In this sample food diary, I'm trying to show that milk caused a delayed reaction one-and-a-half to two hours after eating a meal. Apples apparently cause no symptoms. The chicken sandwich causes an immediate reaction. The hives on the face could be the chicken, wheat (from the bread), or soy from the mayonnaise.

See how easy it is to start to identify your food allergies from a simple piece of paper! See how important it is to write down *everything* you eat—*immediately* after you eat it!

Also, because you may not be getting a well-balanced diet with your new allergy-free diet, go to *www.mypyramidtracker.gov* and record your foods. It will show you what you are missing and give suggestions on how to improve your diet. This is especially important for your children's diet.

Now here's a blank food diary for you to use. Copy it, enlarging it if you like.

Food Diary for_____

Date_____

TIME OF MEAL	FOOD/DRINK/ MEDICINE	TIME OF SYMPTOMS	SYMPTONS

FOODS TO AVOID

In this part of your notebook you will make a list of all the foods you must avoid; be sure to include a list of the many derivatives that foods can be processed into or the different words that might be used to describe a product (see chapter 3). For major allergens, it's easier if you use one page for each allergy. Your food allergies will change; over time you will identify more allergens while simultaneously you'll be able to bring back into your diet foods you once had to avoid.

List of Allowed Foods, Grocery List, and Food Sources

Make up a chart of allowed foods and list all the foods you are permitted to eat. For example, if you can eat rice, include rice cakes, rice crackers, rice cereal, and so on.

Type up a grocery list of foods allowed and make several copies. Put one in your notebook and leave another one in a handy spot so that family members can circle the foods as they are needed. You may want to divide the list into supermarket, health food store, fish market, and fruit stand and list the foods you buy under each section. When I lived in New York City, a block away from the United Nations, there were no supermarkets nearby. I found it exciting to walk out of my apartment and go to the deluxe bakery; the fish store, where the fish monger was an expert on every fish he sold; the fruit and vegetable store, where the owner would take time to help a customer pick out the best fruit or explain how to prepare a new vegetable. There were specialty stores for everything, and little ethnic grocery stores all over the city. I loved it all! I learned so much from the store owners who were always happy to see me.

I walked two to three miles every day, and that was to keep the weight off from eating all those delicious (allergy-free) foods. I developed the idea for keeping a notebook since I walked all over town and couldn't remember later where I had bought the foods I liked.

Finally, make a chart similar to the one below and keep a list of the new foods you like and where you bought the food item (including internet-ordered items). When you go grocery shopping, you can take the entire notebook with you, or just the page with the grocery list on it.

Food Sources

Name of product: _____

Ingredients: _____

_____

_____

_____

Food bought at: _____

Mail-order information: _____

_____

Manufacturer: _____

Website: _____

Address: _____

City: _____State: _____Zip: _____

Telephone: _____

Suggested Uses: _____

_____

MENUS

Create a list of menus to keep in your notebook (see samples in chapter 7). When you plan to go shopping, pick out as many different menus as you wish to shop for and jot down the ingredients. This will help reduce the temptation of eating your former foods.

COOKING SUGGESTIONS AND SUBSTITUTIONS

After reading chapter 5, you might want to begin a list of common food substitutions and new cooking tips you come across. Make this notebook your own "cookbook" so you can turn to whatever section you need just like a cookbook. Also use this section for experimenting with a new ingredient as follows: It's very hard to break out of one's old ways of eating and begin eating unfamiliar foods. It becomes twice as difficult when you have no idea how to cook with the new food. I suggest that you keep a record of all your attempts, along with the ingredient measurements. At some point you'll come up with something good tasting and you will want to be able to duplicate it.

New Ingredients Worksheet

Mango

- Tried to slice it, rather soft. Perhaps it's overripe. There's not much fruit with the large stone.
- Tried it in a fruit salad with bananas, kiwis, strawberries, and seedless grapes. Delicious!
- Tried it with tuna salad; it's too sweet and mushy. Maybe try it with chicken or sliced over a bland fish. Perhaps it would taste all right sliced over fish and then broiled?
- Put it in the blender and pureed it. Great substitute for applesauce. Because of its sweetness, perhaps it would be good in place of bananas in banana bread recipe?
- The mango sauce darkened; next time try a dash of lemon or pineapple juice to prevent it from darkening.
- Used the exact amount of mango sauce for applesauce in tapioca pudding recipe. Actually has a sweeter taste.
- Put it in the blender with water like orange juice. Ugh! Forget it.
- Put it in the blender with other fruits and juices:
    - $\frac{1}{2}$ cup orange juice
    - $\frac{1}{2}$ cup apple juice
    - $\frac{1}{2}$ cup diced mango
    - 1 cup crushed ice
    - 1 cup water

Tastes great!

RECIPE DEVELOPMENT

Once you know what foods you're allergic to, you can turn your attention to creating recipes that will suit your personal needs. You can take your family's favorite recipes and start adapting those using allowed ingredients. You may want to keep a record of the original recipes, the new recipes with their substitutions, and notes on how you liked the changes you made. If you are lucky, the first attempt will taste great. However, you might want to change the ingredients or the instructions further. By keeping a record, you'll know where to start the next time. And, please, please, don't get discouraged if your first attempt doesn't work out. When I first started cooking with allergy-free ingredients, my muffins turned into bouncing rubber balls—fun to play with, but not to eat!

RECIPE DEVELOPMENT WORKSHEET

ORIGINAL RECIPE:
Baking-Powder Biscuits

1 cup all-purpose flour

3 teaspoons baking powder

$^1/_2$ teaspoon salt

5 tablespoons oil

$^3/_4$ cup milk

Preheat the oven to 475°F.

Sift together the dry ingredients. Mix in the oil until finely mixed. Stir in the milk to make a soft dough, which will be a little sticky. Knead on a lightly floured surface for approximately 5 minutes. Press out to $^3/_4$ or 1 inch thick. Cut and bake on a greased pan at 475°F for 10 to 15 minutes, until golden brown.

NEW RECIPE:
Baking-Powder Biscuits

1 $^1/_4$ cups potato starch

$^1/_4$ cup brown rice or barley flour

4 teaspoons baking powder

$^1/_2$ teaspoon salt

$^1/_3$ cup shortening or oil

$^1/_4$ to 1 cup oat or sesame milk

Preheat the oven to 475°F.

Sift together the dry ingredients. Mix in the shortening or oil until finely mixed. Stir in enough liquid to make a soft dough. Knead on a lightly floured (barley or rice flour) surface for approximately 5 minutes. Press out to $^3/_4$ or 1 inch thick. Cut and bake on a greased pan at 475°F for 10 to 15 minutes, until golden brown.

RECIPIES

You can have either a large notebook which also includes recipes. Or, you can have a separate notebook with recipes you develop and acquire from the internet (there are many, many sites). Thirty years ago I developed this cookbook by starting out with a notebook and dividers and creating recipes for my family. You might want to start by using the same titles as I have in this book, or create your own. It's very empowering to create and write recipes. Who knows, you might end up with an allergy-free cookbook too!

MISCELLANEOUS

In this section you might want to keep questions to talk over with your doctor, and keep notes on your doctor's suggestions.

You can use this section for anything actually; keep articles you find interesting from the internet, or keep all your medical documents and test reports here.

I would recommend that you keep a to-do list here on steps you need to take to begin your diet.

3.

Identifying Allergens

When I started rewriting this book, I thought, *Aha! I can eliminate this chapter*, because the new Food Allergy Labeling and Consumer Protection Act of 2004 (FALCPA) has been in effect since the beginning of 2006. Briefly, it requires food manufacturers to clearly identify their product if it contains any of the eight major food allergens listed under this law. These eight major foods or food groups tend to cause 90 percent of allergic reactions in the United States.

Under FALCPA, the law identifies these eight major foods or food groups as milk, egg, wheat, soybean, peanut, tree nuts, fish, and shellfish. If you want to find out more about the Food Labeling Act, just search on the internet for "FALCPA."

Each food manufacturer can vary how the label is presented as long as it follows the requirements of the law. Food manufacturers can label their package in one of two ways:

1. In a list of ingredients, followed by the name of the major food allergen in parenthesis if it is not in the ingredient name. For example: Enriched flour (**wheat** flour), whey (**milk**), **egg**

or

2. Immediately after or adjacent to the list of ingredients, the food manufacturer puts the words "Contains" followed by the name of the allergenic food.

For example:

> Contains: Milk, Egg, Wheat

or

> Allergy Statement: This product contains
> wheat and milk. It is manufactured on equipment that
> may come in contact with peanuts or their oil.

Now there are some good labels and some really useless labels. First, here is a clear label:

> **WHITE WHOLE WHEAT BREAD**
> Ingredients: Whole Wheat Flour, Water, Sugar, Fresh
> Buttermilk (Milk), Soy Oil (Soy), Fresh Butter (Milk), Fresh
> Eggs, Yeast, Salt Dough Conditioner, Corn Meal.
> Made on Shared Equipment with Tree Nuts.

Now, here's a totally useless label for Chocolate Fudge by a real gourmet confectionary company:

> **GOURMET CHOCOLATE FUDGE**
> Ingredients: Sugar, Corn Syrup, Chocolate Liquor,
> Cream, Butter, Coconut Oil, Potassium Sorbate.
> ALLERGY STATEMENT: this product may contain or
> have proteins derived from milk, eggs, fish, crustacean
> shellfish, tree nuts, wheat, peanuts and/or soybeans.

Do you honestly believe the confectionary company has the money to add lobster, crab, or shrimp to chocolate fudge? I don't think lobster or halibut in my fudge would taste so great. The purpose of that label was to have a generic label printed for any product. It helped the company save money, but it totally defeated the purpose of the new law! So, I guess I'll write a letter of complaint to my congressional representative.

EIGHT MAJOR FOOD GROUPS

One of the biggest problems in determining what foods you should avoid is identifying the original source of an ingredient. There's so much you need to know so you won't unknowingly get sick. For example, if you're trying to avoid corn and you scan a packaged-food label for this ingredient, you may not find it. However, the label may list a derivative of corn, such as dextrose. Corn's derivatives are not required to be identified as corn.

I've included lists of alternative ingredients for milk, eggs, wheat, soy, corn, shellfish, tree nuts, and peanuts. The following sections will help you in deciphering labels that aren't beneficial to you.

WHEAT-CONTAINING FOODS

Wheat is one of the eight major foods, here are some other names for wheat.

- all-purpose flour
- bran
- bread crumbs
- bread flour
- bulgur
- cake flour
- cracked wheat flour
- cracker meal and crumbs
- durum
- enriched flour
- farina
- gluten flour
- hydrolyzed vegetable protein (hvp)*
- flour
- graham crackers and crumbs

- graham flour
- malt*
- malt syrup*
- monosodium glutamate*
- pastry flour
- phosphated flour
- semolina
- wheat
- wheat germ
- wheat starch
- wheat flour
- white flour
- whole wheat flour

* Gluten and/or wheat is often present, but not always.

* Kamut and Spelt are closely related to wheat and should be omitted until separately tested.

CORN-CONTAINING FOODS

Although corn is not listed in the top eight food allergens, I strongly believe it causes major food reactions simply because you are exposed to it every day in so many different ways. Remember, one way you develop an allergic reaction is through repeated exposure. You are being exposed to corn every day if you eat processed food. I find it's almost impossible to eliminate corn in a modern diet.

When looking for corn derivatives on a food label, you should know that corn can be processed into the forms of:

* Corn syrup
* Corn meal

* Corn oil
* Corn starch or corn flour

Corn can be further processed into:

* alcohol
* caramel color
* dextrin
* dextrose
* fructose
* lactic acid
* modified food starch*

* maltodextrins
* mannitol
* sorbitol

* Modified food starch can also be derived from other ingredients, such as tapioca, potatoes, or wheat.

As you can see, this is a formidable list and will require a lot of detection work if you are trying to eliminate corn from your diet. It does not mean, however, that you are automatically allergic to all these items if you are allergic to corn. You may be allergic to some of these products and not to others. Only by testing each food can you tell to which items you are allergic. I have many reactions to corn. I can't tolerate corn puffs, corn tortillas (not even the smell), corn oil, or corn meal. I can have only Pepsi or occasionally Coke, absolutely no other brands of soda. I can eat Green Giant canned corn without any problems at all. I believe this is due to the high heat used during the canning process; it destroys some of the protein.

Identifying Foods Containing Corn

To further help you in the difficult task of avoiding corn, below is a partial list of some of the many foods in which corn may be used:

- baby foods
- bacon
- baking mixes
- baking powders
- batters for frying
- beers
- bleached wheat flours
- bourbon and other whiskeys
- bread and pastries
- cakes
- candies
- carbonated beverages
- catsups
- cereals
- cheeses
- chili
- chop suey
- chow mein
- coffee, instant
- colas
- cookies
- confectioners' sugar
- cream pies
- dextrose

- eggnog
- fish, prepared and processed
- foods, fried
- frostings
- fruits, canned and frozen
- fruit juices
- fruit pies
- frying fats
- gelatin desserts
- gin
- ginger ale
- glucose and fructose products
- graham crackers
- grape juice
- gravies
- grits
- gums, chewing
- hams, cured
- Harvard beets
- ices and sherbet
- ice creams
- jams and jellies
- leavening agents and yeasts
- liquors
- margarines and shortenings
- meats, processed and cold cuts
- milk, in paper cartons*

- monosodium glutamate
- peanut butter and canned peanuts
- pickles
- powdered sugar
- puddings and custards
- salad dressings
- salt
- sandwich spreads
- sauces for sundaes, meats,
    fish, etc.
- sausages
- soft drinks
- spaghetti
- soups, thickened and creamed,
- soy milk
- syrups, corn
- teas, instant
- tortillas
- vanillin
- vegetables, canned, creamed,
  and frozen
- vinegar, distilled
- waffles
- wines

* The paper carton contains corn,
  not the milk.

EGG-CONTAINING FOODS

With the new law, egg must be identified on all food products, which helps consumers a lot. Eggs are found in many processed foods. For example, egg whites may be brushed on breads, rolls, pretzels, and other baked goods to give a glazed effect. Wine, beer, real root beer, coffee, bouillon, and consommé may be clarified with egg. Most cholesterol-reducing "egg replacers" have egg whites, even a little egg yolk, as an ingredient. The exceptions to this are special allergy-free brand egg replacers such as Jolly Joan Egg Replacer.

Egg is present if the label indicates any of the following:

* *albumin*
* *globulin*
* *livetin*
* *ovomucim*

* *ovomucoid*
* *ovovitellin*
* *powdered or dried egg*

* *silico albuminate*
* *vitellin*
* *yolk*

MILK-CONTAINING FOODS

Milk is now clearly labeled on all packaged food. Labels may contain one of the following names if a product contains milk or milk protein:

* *casein*
* *caseinate*
* *curds*
* *lactose*

* *lactalbumin*
* *lactoglobulin*
* *milk solids*
* *potassium caseinate*

* *sodium caseinate*
* *whey*

Milk has many different proteins, but casein and whey are the most allergy-causing proteins. The whey fraction, which contains lactalbumin and beta lactoglobulin, causes the most reactions. However, you should test for both fractions. Individuals who are allergic only to the whey (and not the casein) may be able to tolerate goat's milk since the whey fraction differs from that in cow's milk. Powdered, boiled, or evaporated cow's milk may also be tolerated since the whey protein is changed by the heating process.

Those individuals allergic to whey will have to *avoid*:

- cottage cheese
- soft processed cheeses

Those individuals allergic to whey *may be able to tolerate*:

- Cheddar
- Edam
- Gruyère
- Parmesan
- Romano
- Swiss
- Other hard cheeses

If you're not allergic to whey protein, you may be able to tolerate ricotta cheese, which contains whey, a byproduct of another cheese.

Casein remains stable during the heating process, so powdered, evaporated, or boiled milk cannot be consumed. The casein is similar both in goat's milk and cow's milk, so both must be avoided. Even nondairy creamers, imitation processed cheeses, imitation cream cheese, imitation sour cream, and soybean-based ice cream may contain casein. Therefore all labels must be read carefully.

Rennet

Rennet is used in making cheese. It contains two active components, rennin and pepsin. These enzymes have the properties of clotting or curdling milk.

Rennet can come from animal, vegetable, or microbial sources. Usually, rennet is obtained from the stomach of young mammals living on milk, especially from the inner lining of the fourth, or true, stomach of milk-fed calves. According to Trader Joe's, they use rennet from the calf of a lamb.

Trader Joe's has written an informational page about the different types of rennet used in its cheese. Each cheese company uses different types of rennet when producing its own brand of cheese. You can check Trader Joe's website for information under FAQ at *www.Traderjoes.com.*

SOY-CONTAINING FOODS

Soybeans can be processed into so many different forms, especially "imitation" foods, like meat, sour cream, or nuts. It can be flaked, powdered, spun, and extruded. Soy albumin acts as a whipping and foaming agent and can be a low-cost egg white replacer.

Soybeans can be made into tempeh, a fermented soy food used as a meat substitute, which has been inoculated with a mold during processing. It can be made into tofu, a curdled soybean milk, or into miso, a thick, salty soybean paste used in concentrated soup bases, sauces, salad dressings, and spreads.

Soybeans can also be processed into:

• *Flour*	• *Oil*	• *Soy isolates*
• *Grits*	• *Margarine*	• *Textured vegetable*
• *Bran*	• *Lecithin*	*protein*
• *Kernels*	• *Soy albumin*	

Some processed foods that may contain soybeans are:

Bakery goods such as vegetable oil, flour, and protein fillers in some breads, rolls, cakes, pastries, packaged mixes, and crackers.

Sauces such as soy, oriental, gravies, Worcestershire, etc.

Cereals may include lecithin.

Salad dressings: used as an oil, a thickener, and an emulsifier for mayonnaise.

Meats: cold cuts, luncheon meats, sausages, hot dogs, hamburgers, Hamburger Helper, and other such mixes may contain soybeans as protein fillers or supplements.

Soy isolates may be pumped into whole cuts of meat by injection or massage. Since soy retains the fat and moisture, it reduces shrinkage. In the past, no indication of such treatment was on the label.

Candies: soy flour and oil are used in some hard candies, nut candies, and caramels; lecithin is used to prevent drying and to emulsify the fats.

Milk substitutes such as soy milk, non-dairy products, packaged mixes, and margarines. Bakeries use them instead of cow's milk. Infant formulas may contain soybean flour and soy milk powder.

Desserts: ice cream, iced milk, sherbet, etc.

Diet aids such as soy liquid proteins.

Soups: soybeans are used as a substitute for wheat to thicken.

Vegetables: soy sprouts, soybeans, Chinese food.

Nuts: oil is used to roast nuts; soy nuts look like peanuts.

Pastas such as soybean noodles, macaroni, spaghetti.

Shortenings, margarines, and butter substitutes.

Soy cheese: may be found in some processed cheeses.

Fried products: corn chips, potato chips, French fried potatoes, processed fish, and other substances are often fried in soy oil.

Drinks: coffee substitutes, dry lemonade mixes.

Soy milk infant formulas.

Canned fish: tuna, sardines, and other fish are often packed in soy oil.

Popcorn might have soybean-flavored butter substitute.

Molasses listed as an ingredient in a product may contain soy.

TREE NUTS

When the Food Allergy Labeling Consumer Protection Act (FALCPA) was enacted, the law stated that *all* tree nuts must be stated on a food label. Peanuts are a legume and are in a different biological food family. Check with your doctor to see if you can have peanuts. Water chestnuts are not tree nuts.

Tree nuts include:

- Almonds
- Artificial nuts*
- Brazil nuts
- Cashews
- Chestnuts
- Filberts (Hazelnuts)
- Hickory nuts
- Macadamia nuts
- Pecans
- Pine nuts
- Pistachios
- Walnuts, both black walnuts and English walnuts

Note: Avoid all sources of tree nut proteins:

- Almond paste
- Artificial flavorings
- Artificial nuts*
- Baking mixes
- Barbecue sauce
- Cakes
- Cereal
- Cereal bars
- Chinese foods
- Cookies
- Crackers
- Deli salads
- Dessert spreads
- Doughnuts
- Frozen desserts
- Frozen yogurts
- Gianduja, a nut mixture with chocolate
- Granola bars
- Ice cream
- Marzipan
- Muffins
- Natural nut flavors, such as almond extract
- Nut butters
- Nut-flavored coffee
- Nut-flavored liquors
- Pesto
- Pralines
- Salad dressings
- Sundae toppings
- Trail mix
- Worcestershire sauce

* Artificial nuts can be peanuts that have been deflavored and reflavored with a nut.

FISH

If you have a fish allergy, you must talk to your doctor and get instructions regarding whether or not you can eat other biological families of fish. Due to cross-contamination of different types of fish when they are packaged, or when they are cooked at a restaurant, it is usually wise to avoid all types of fish. This depends on the severity of your reaction. If you have a very severe reaction to fish, you should probably avoid shellfish too since shellfish, such as shrimp, is contaminated with fish protein due to being in close proximity with fish or from being cooked on the same grill. If the cook fries fish in the same oil as potatoes, such as for fish and chips, you have to avoid anything fried at that particular restaurant.

SHELLFISH OR CRUSTACEANS

Shellfish allergies are the most common food allergies among adults in America. What's interesting is that the symptoms usually don't begin until people become adults. Maybe this is because kids don't eat lobster, crab, and shrimp as often as adults do.

Shellfish, along with nuts, are the most common food cause of anaphylactic shock. I developed my first reaction to shrimp when I was eighteen, and had hives and swelling of my mouth and throat. The next time I had shrimp I had a severe anaphylactic reaction.

Crustaceans

People who are allergic to crustaceans will need to avoid the following:

- Crab
- Crayfish (crawfish or crawdads)
- Langoustines
- Lobster
- Prawns
- Shrimp
- Sea Urchin

Shellfish is not a common hidden ingredient, so reading the label will be easy. Shellfish can be found in a few foods, such as surimi, an imitation shellfish that contains shellfish extract for flavoring. Shellfish can also be found in some sauces such as Worcestershire sauce, salad dressings, and other prepared sauces. Just make sure to read the label very carefully.

Shellfish and Restaurants

Shellfish is a common condiment in Asian food, such as Thai Kapi, Nam Prik, Mam Tom, and Chinese dried shellfish. Japanese restaurants are known for their great sushi bars and communal grill-style restaurants. Unfortunately there is a high risk of cross-contamination.

Another cause of cross-contamination is when restaurants cook fish and shellfish on the same grill, or fry potatoes and shrimp in the same oil.

Other menu terms that might indicate shellfish include:

- Bouillabase (a French fish soup)
- Cioppino
- A l'Americaine (a French sauce often served with lobster or other shellfish)

- Crevette (the French term for *shrimp*)
- Scampi
- Ceviche (fish or shellfish cooked by marinating in an acidic citrus-based marinade)
- Etouffee
- Gumbo
- Jambalaya

Note. Prawns are different from shrimp and can be distinguished by the gill structure; however in America, the terms prawn and shrimp are generally used interchangeably. In America, the word prawn is also loosely used to describe any large shrimp, especially those that come fifteen (or fewer) to the pound, also known as "king prawns." In England, the word prawn is almost always used regardless of size.

Mollusks

People with shellfish allergies have a propensity to develop an allergic reaction to mollusks since the shellfish and mollusks have similar proteins. Your doctor will tell you if you need to eliminate mollusks as well. Mollusks are not part of the major eight food allergens that are included under FALCPA.

Foods to Avoid if Allergic to Mollusks

- Abalone
- Calimari (Squid)
- Clams
- Cockles
- Escargot (Snails)
- Limpets
- Octopus
- Oysters
- Mussels
- Quahogs
- Scallops
- Whelks

PEANUT-CONTAINING FOODS

Did you know that peanuts are not nuts, but belong to the legume family, which includes soybean, peas, and other beans?

Did you know that peanuts are the most common cause of death from food allergies? About one-third of people with peanut allergies have fatal or near-fatal anaphylactic reactions. Even with minimal contact, peanuts can cause serious reactions. Over the last five to ten years, there has been a sharp increase in peanut allergies, particularly in children. This is occurring not only in the United States but in Australia and England. Although there is no definitive cause for this reason, scientists speculate that parents are giving children peanuts too soon. Another is that there is an increase in the use of soy formula, which is in the same biological family as peanuts. I believe over the last twenty-five years there has been a better acceptance of food allergies by doctors, followed by better and easier diagnostic tests. When more doctors treat food allergies, the symptoms get reported more often.

The smell of peanuts or even secondhand contact has been well documented in causing an allergic reaction. It's very easy for kids to eat peanut butter and jelly sandwiches and then not wash their hands adequately. If they touch a peanut-sensitive child, it can cause the allergic child to experience any type of symptom, including anaphylactic shock.

Peanuts are very inexpensive compared to other nuts; they can be deflavored of their peanut taste and flavored with that of a nut.

Peanuts can be found in some of the following foods.

- Asian foods
- Baking mixes
- Breads
- Cereals
- Chili
- Chocolate
- Chocolate ice cream
- Cookies
- Crackers
- Egg rolls
- Energy bars
- Flavorings
- Frozen desserts
- Granola
- Ice cream
- Milk formulas
- Mixed nuts
- Mandalona—a nut substitute derived from peanut meal
- Mortadella
- Muffins
- Nougats
- Nut butters
- Nutella spread
- Pastries
- Peanut butter
- Peanut oil
- Pesto
- Sauces—often used as a thickener
- Salad dressing
- Satay sauces
- Seasoning
- Soups
- Vegetarian burgers

4.

Allergy-Free Shopping

Now that you know what foods you must eliminate from your diet, you need to prepare a list of foods you can have. Because you want to avoid your allergens and the additives often present in packaged foods, it is best to shop for foods that are more natural and less processed. Make sure you read the labels of packaged foods *each time* you purchase them because product ingredients can change without notice. In addition, try different brands of food products since one brand may be better tolerated than another.

Although you may be able to buy most or all of the foods you need at a grocery store, it is a good idea to locate a well-stocked health food store near your home, like Whole Foods Market or Trader Joe's. Many health food stores offer chemical- and additive-free meats, poultry, fish, and produce as well as a variety of ingredients that are difficult to find at a regular supermarket. Some may have personnel who can give you additional suggestions of new ingredients or food products. If you are still having trouble locating an ingredient or product, check the internet. You may be able to contact the manufacturer directly through the internet. Before you make up your own grocery list, read the section on cooking tips and substitutions, the menus, and recipes to determine which foods make the most sense for your particular diet and tastes.

The following list is a sample of the foods *allowed* on the allergy-free diet:

Baking Products

- Baking powder (preferably corn-free)
- Baking soda
- Carob or cocoa
- Coconut
- Cream of tartar
- Egg-replacer, such as Jolly Joan brand
- Tapioca, instant
- Vanilla, pure

Beverages

- Almond nut milk
- Apple juice (100% pure unsweetened)
- Apricot juice (100% pure)
- Bottled spring water
- Carrot juice (100% pure)
- Celery juice (100% pure)
- Goat's milk, canned evaporated, fresh or powdered such as Meyenberg brand
- Grape juice (100% pure unsweetened)
- Grapefruit juice (100% pure)
- Imagine Foods Rice Dream Vanilla Dairy Substitute *
- Orange juice (100% pure)
- Pacific Foods of Oregon Almond Dairy Substitute *
- Pacific Foods of Oregon Original Dairy Substitute *
- Pear juice (100% pure)
- Pineapple juice (100% pure unsweetened)
- Rice Dream Organic Original *
- Tomato juice (100% pure)

* Read labels on these products to make sure ingredients havn't changed.

Flours, Grains, Noodles, and Thickeners

- Agar
- Almond meal
- Amaranth flour
- Arrowroot starch
- Barley flour
- Brown Rice Flour Superfine, a thickening agent, through Authentic Foods
- Buckwheat flour
- Buckwheat groats
- Buckwheat soba noodles, some by Eden Foods
- Corn flour
- Corn starch
- Chick-pea (Garbanzo) flour
- Garfava flour (a blend of garbanzo flour and fava flour available through Authentic Foods Gluten-Free Supermarket
- Gelatin (made from beef and/or pork)
- Gluten free blends, such as blends by Authentic Foods
- Jerusalem Artichoke flour, by such companies as De Boles
- Kamut flour
- Kudzu root starch
- Millet flour
- Oat flour
- Oatmeal
- Rolled oats
- Potato flour (cooked)
- Potato starch (uncooked)
- Quinoa
- Rice
- Rice noodles
- Rice flour
- Rye flour
- Sorghum flour (gluten-free)
- Spelt flour
- Sweet Rice Flour Superfine, a thickening agent, through Authentic Foods
- Tapioca, instant
- Tapioca starch flour
- White corn flour, superfine
- White rice flour, superfine
- Xanthan gum

Fruits and Vegetables

- Alfalfa sprouts
- Apples
- Applesauce
- Apricots
- Artichoke
- Asparagus
- Avocado
- Bamboo shoots
- Banana
- Beets
- Blackberries
- Black-eyed peas
- Blueberries
- Broccoli
- Brussels sprouts
- Cabbage
- Cantaloupe and other melons
- Carrots
- Cauliflower
- Celery
- Cherries
- Chick-peas (garbanzo)
- Coconut (fresh)
- Collard greens
- Cranberries
- Cucumber
- Currants
- Dates
- Eggplant
- Endive
- Figs
- Grapefruit
- Grapes
- Green beans
- Kale
- Kelp and other Sea Vegetables
- Kidney beans
- Kiwi
- Lamb's quarters
- Leek
- Lemon
- Lentils
- Lettuce, all types
- Lima beans
- Lime
- Mango
- Mung beans
- Mushrooms
- Muskmelon
- Navy beans
- Nectarine
- Orange
- Papaya
- Parsnip
- Peach
- Pear
- Persimmon
- Pineapple
- Pinto beans
- Plum
- Potatoes
- Pumpkin
- Radish
- Raisins
- Raspberries
- Rhubarb
- Rutabaga
- Spinach
- Squash, all types
- Strawberries
- Sweet potatoes
- Swiss chard

- Tangerine
- Tomato
- Turnip

- Water chestnut
- Watermelon
- Yam

- Zucchini

Meat, Poultry, and Fish

- Beef
- Buffalo
- Chicken
- Cornish hen
- Duck

- Goose
- Lamb
- Pheasant
- Pork
- Quail

- Rabbit
- Turkey
- Eggs, if tolerated

Miscellaneous

- 100% Soba Noodles (all buckwheat)
- Banana Chips
- Blue corn chips (sometimes less allergenic than the yellow corn chips)
- Cashew nut butter (if not tree nut allergic)

- Imitation Catsup * by Hain Pure Food
- Carrot chips * by Hain Pure Food
- Imitation mayonnaise * by Hain Pure Food or
- Canola mayonnaise by Trader Joe's or Whole Foods *
- Potato chips in safflower oil

- Rice cakes
- Rice crackers, some by Eden Foods *
- Rice sticks
- Vegetable chips, some by Eden Foods *
- Vinegar, all types such as apple, balsamic or grape

*Read labels on these products to make sure ingredients haven't changed.

Nuts and Seeds

- Almond **
- Brazil nuts **
- Cashews **
- Filberts **
- Hazelnuts **
- Macadamia nuts **
- Pecans **
- Pine nuts **

- Pistachios, undyed **
- Pumpkin seeds
- Sesame seeds
- Sunflower seeds
- Tahini butter
  (sesame seed butter)
- Walnuts **

** Avoid if you have a tree nut allergy

Oils and Fats

- Almond oil
- Avocado oil
- Butter
- Canola oil
- Coconut oil
- Safflower oil
- Sesame oil

- Sunflower oil
- Walnut oil

Note: If you have a tree nut allergy, use heat processed oils, not cold-pressed oils, which still have nut protein in them.

Sweeteners

- Amasake (brown rice)
- Barley malt,
  some by Eden Foods
- Beet sugar
- Cane sugar
- Date sugar
- Honey, all types
- Maple sugar
- Maple syrup
- Rice syrup

Seasonings

- Allspice
- Anise
- Basil
- Bay leaf
- Cardamom
- Celery seeds
- Cloves
- Coriander
- Curry powder
- Dill
- Fennel, ground
- Fennel, seeds
- Ginger
- Mace
- Marjoram
- Nutmeg
- Oregano
- Parsley
- Rosemary
- Saffron
- Sage
- Savory
- Sea Salt
- Thyme

* Read labels on these products to make sure ingredients haven't changed.

Apples

Some apples may be covered with a coating and should be avoided. Even the organic apples at local health food stores have shellac on them. Check with the grocer to find out if any are not waxed. Try your local farmer's market where you can get fresh, locally grown fruits and vegetables that might not have any shellac.

The FDA writes that apple packers or repackers must use the phrase "coated with food-grade animal-based wax, to maintain freshness," or "coated with food-grade vegetable-, petroleum-, beeswax-, and/or shellac-based wax or resin, to maintain freshness." It further states the term *resin* may be substituted for the term *shellac*.

See if applesauce free of preservatives and sugars are tolerated; if not, make your own applesauce (see page 260). Drink only pure apple juice free of sugar and preservatives (such as After the Fall, which offers dozen of juices).

Arrowroot

During my younger days, I'm sure I read somewhere that arrowroot was a healthier alternative. Honestly, though, until I sat down to write about it, I couldn't have told you whether it *is* a root, and whether it's the root of an arrow or a root *shaped* like an arrow. And yet, there it is, always on my spice rack. Arrowroot is, in fact, a powder made from the ground root of a *Marantha arundinaceous*, a plant indigenous to the West Indies. The starch is extracted from rhizomes that have been growing for six to twelve months. The most popular explanation of how arrowroot got its name is from the Arawak Indians who called it *aru aru*, meaning "food of food." They used the starch to draw out the toxins from wounds made by poisonous arrows.

Considered easier on the stomach than other forms of starch, arrow-root contains calcium and carbohydrates (less than in cornstarch) as well as other nutrients, making it an effective digestive and nutrition aid. In fact, in my supermarket, arrowroot biscuit packages feature happy, smiling babies on the box. In the kitchen there are several advantages to using arrowroot. First, it's a more powerful thickening agent than wheat flour. Substitute two teaspoons of arrowroot for one tablespoon of all-purpose flour. Or, substitute one-for-one in recipes calling for cornstarch.

Second, arrowroot is flavorless and becomes clear when cooked. Unlike cornstarch, it doesn't dull the appearance of sauces, fruit gels, or ice cream.

Third, arrowroot mixtures thicken at a lower temperature than mixtures made with flour. And unlike cornstarch, it doesn't liquefy the sauce when it is reheated again.

As a replacement for cornstarch, it can be located in the spice section of the grocery store. It is also available at health food stores or through the internet.

Baking Powder

Baking powder is a leavening agent for baked goods that creates the necessary gas for cakes, breads, and muffins. It is a mixture of chemical-leavening agents with starch. The starch in most common baking powder is corn starch. One product, Hain Pure Food Featherweight brand, uses potato starch in place of corn starch. Ener-G Foods creates a corn-free baking powder using calcium carbonate. The Featherweight product is available in the diet section of your grocery store, and Ener-G Foods are in your health food store.

Bananas

I buy extra bananas and let them ripen. I peel them and put them in a freezer bag. Whenever you want to make a beverage, cut the frozen bananas up in one-inch pieces and put them slowly into a blender. It makes any blender shake taste like a frosty. When you have two or three overripe bananas, make a banana cake, banana bread, banana muffins, or banana oatmeal cookies. See the index for the recipe page numbers. For children, there are Frozen Bananas that taste like banana ice cream. It's quite messy when kids take gooey honey or mushy nut butter and smear it on wet, frozen banana pieces that have started to thaw out and are slightly wet and feels slimly. They simply love it!

Of course, you can insert a popsicle stick before you freeze them and use a knife or spoon to apply the nut butter or honey. But that wouldn't be as much fun for the kids. Surprisingly, it still remains one of my reader's favorite recipe requests.

Broth/Stock

Most canned broth or stock contains additives, such as MSG, garlic, or onions, so use only homemade broth or stock (see chapter 12). I've had patients experience reactions similar to MSG symptoms, and when I've called the company, they state there's no MSG added. They comment, though, they have no control over what other companies add to the products prior to their purchasing the ingredients for the broth.

Buckwheat

Although buckwheat belongs to the same biological family as rhubarb, it makes a good grain-free substitute for wheat. It is available as flour or groats. Since the flavor is strong, you might want to combine it with another grain or thickener. You can also buy white buckwheat flour, which doesn't have such a *strong* flavor.

Butter

Although butter is a milk product, it is mostly oil with a small amount of whey. Butter is made up of one ingredient whereas margarine can have ten to fifteen ingredients. Very few people who are allergic to milk are allergic to butter. In fact, in all the years that I saw patients with food allergies, only one person had a reaction to butter. So while you are testing for food allergies, use butter instead of margarine when you are baking. Use canola, safflower, or sunflower oil at other times. Once you have completed all your food allergy tests, you can look for a healthier brand of margarine suitable for baking.

Carob Powder

Carob is known as an alternative to chocolate. Carob powder can be substituted equally in place of cocoa in any recipe. Carob powder and milk-free carob bars can be found in all health food stores or through the internet.

The carob tree is a member of the legume (pea, soy, peanut) family, so first determine if you are allergic to carob. You can mix a tablespoon with some applesauce or a safe beverage and see if you have a reaction. Follow the guidelines for testing foods in chapter 1.

Catsup

Did you know that catsup can also be spelled ketchup or even catchup? Regular catsup contains one-third sugar, with most common catsup containing high fructose corn sweetener. Instead of my recommending a specific brand name, go to *www.thenibble.com/reviews/main/condiments/ketchup*. The author has tasted and reviewed more than forty brands of tomato and non-tomato based ketchups! The article is excellent with more than seventeen pages of information about different brands of catsup.

Coconut

Most coconut found in a regular grocery store contains sugar or corn sweeteners and preservatives. Unsweetened coconut is available at health food stores, through Ener-G Foods, or through the internet. To make coconut milk, mix in the blender for a few seconds with water.

Date Sugar

This sugar is made of finely ground dehydrated dates and can be used as you would brown sugar. I would recommend using about two-thirds cup regular sugar if you substitute since date sugar is very sweet. Although it does not have that smooth melting effect like other sugars, it can still be used as a sweetener in beverages, cereals, and desserts and baked goods. You can order date sugar through *www.bobsredmill.com* plus get additional recipes using alternative flours.

Egg Replacer

The best known brand that is guaranteed free of eggs is Jolly Joan egg replacer by Ener-G Foods (*www.ener-g.com*), which is available at almost all health food stores. There are other brands of egg replacers, so look through the internet to see what ingredients you want in your egg replacer.

Fish

The FDA gave manufacturers of processed seafood products broad guidelines when they prepare their food labels. If the manufacturer is unable to use the same type of fish due to seasonal shortages or other reasons, the fish may still be listed, even if it's not always used in the product. They must simply state "contains one or more of the following." Nor does each fish need to be listed in descending order of predominance.

Some fish and shellfish are dipped into solutions of antibiotics or other preservatives to prevent spoilage. For example, fish and shellfish may be treated with polyphosphates to prevent the frozen fish from dripping a lot as it thaws. Unfortunately, the effect of all polyphosphates treatment is to increase the weight of the fish by retaining water. This chemical does not penetrate the product and can be rinsed off.

Flour

There are dozens of wheat substitutes, such as oats, rice, potato starch, buckwheat, quinoa, spelt, kamut, and tapioca starch. Arrowhead Mills, Ener-G Foods, and Bob's Red Mill supply these wheat-substitute flours. There are dozens of sites on the internet that sell wheat alternatives.

Fruits

Use fresh fruit or fruit canned in its own juice. Avoid canned fruit with heavy or light syrup, as these usually contain corn syrup. Dole packs pineapple in its own juice.

Honey

Some commercial honeys come from sugar-fed bees and may cause reactions in people who are sensitive to cane or beet sugar. If possible, buy locally produced honey so you can find out how the bees are fed. You'll also have a chance to try different types of honey. See page 82 for directions on substituting honey for sugar.

Juices

Use unsweetened juices such as apple, pineapple, or grape. Avoid lemonade, soft drinks, and other sweetened beverages. After the Fall products include a great variety of acceptable juices.

Maple Sugar

In place of cane or beet sugar, maple sugar can be used. It is more expensive than other sugars but is much sweeter and a smaller amount is required. Order pure maple sugar through the internet or check the health food stores.

Maple Syrup

Use only pure maple syrup. Be sure to read labels carefully, as cane or beet is added to some brands.

Mayonnaise

There are different types of mayonnaise that are free of soybean and/or eggs. Spectrum makes several types of mayonnaise; one that is free of both soybeans, and eggs (*www.spectrumorganics.com*).

Meats and Poultry

Do not use processed, smoked, or cured meats (such as hot dogs, bologna, or bacon). They often contain cereal, milk, corn sugar, soybean, food coloring, and additives. Do not use frozen turkey that has been basted since it usually contains milk, soybean or corn. Fresh meats, fish, and poultry are best; organic is even better.

Milk

Almond nut milk, if tolerated, coconut milk, rice milk, goat's milk, water, or pure juice can be used in place of cow's milk. Jackson-Mitchell, Inc. has fresh, canned, or evaporated goat's milk under the name Meyenberg.

Nut and Seed Butter

There are many nut and seed butters available. Try MaraNatha products at *www.maranathanutbutters.com*. Again, if you are allergic to peanuts, you most likely will have to avoid all nut butters or seed butter products due to cross-contamination. If you can find nuts without any cross-contamination, you can make your own nut butter.

Oils

Use heat processed, not cold press canola, safflower, or sunflower oil in place of corn or soybean oil. There are many good brands available at both supermarkets and health food stores.

Paper Goods

If you have an allergy to corn, it's important to note that plastic food wrappers, waxed paper cartons for milk and some juices, paper cups, and wax-coated paper plates are dusted with cornstarch to prevent sticking.

Potato Chips

Use potato chips that are free of additives. For example, potato chips that contain only potatoes, safflower oil or sunflower oil, and sea salt.

Rice Cakes

You can use rice cakes or rice crackers as bread substitutes. They are available at health food stores and through the internet.

Sea Salt

Use sea salt, as most packaged salt may contain sugar. It is added to regular salt to hold down the salt as it goes down the conveyor belt. Sea salt is all natural and has a much larger size crystal. So when using sea salt, you need to *double* the amount of sea salt in place of regular salt.

Sweeteners

In the first edition of this book, I did not use cane or beet sugar since there were so many other healthy sweeteners. I prefer using honey, maple sugar, maple syrup, date sugar, or rice syrup. However, since honey can now cost eight dollars for four ounces, and date sugar costs about six dollars a pound, I have included sugar as an alternative if the other sweeteners are too expensive. My thought, however, is that you won't be baking every day and so you can buy some type of healthier sweetener. Talk to staff at your health food store.

Tree Nuts

If tree nuts are tolerated, use freshly shelled nuts or raw and unprocessed nuts. Some dry-roasted nuts contain additives and preservatives. However, read each label carefully; it will state exactly what it contains and what other common food allergens are processed in the same plant. If you are allergic to peanuts, you most likely will have to avoid all nut products due to cross-contamination.

Vanilla

Use fresh vanilla bean or *pure* vanilla extract.

Vegetables

Discard any outer leaves, peels, skins, or shells to reduce pesticide residue. Some vegetables may be treated with mold inhibitors or fumigated, and red potatoes may be dyed, so check with your grocer.

Xanthan Gum

This is available through the internet or from Ener-G Foods. Compare the prices since they vary considerably on the internet.

5.

Cooking Suggestions
and Substitutions

Although you will be giving up some foods because of allergies, you will most likely want to continue offering meals to your family that you have traditionally prepared. By learning to substitute allergy-free ingredients, you can still enjoy most of your old-time favorites, and with the help of the recipe section in part 2, you may discover new dishes to savor. At first avoiding an ingredient such as wheat or corn may seem almost impossible until you investigate some of the many substitutes available, such as barley, oats, potato starch, and tapioca flour. Of course, there may be some adjustments to make in the amount of alternative flour you substitute or perhaps in the cooking time or temperature, but with a little effort, you'll soon be an expert at wheat-free or soy-free cooking.

You will have to experiment with new ingredients and perhaps even create new recipes. If you and your family think of this as a sort of cooking adventure, you will find it easier to overcome some of the frustrations caused by the changes in your dietary habits. Some substitutions will not affect the taste of a new recipe, but others will produce a different taste, which may take some time to get used to. You may even make some changes in your diet that taste better.

In this chapter you will learn about the many different substitutes available for most common food allergens and how to adjust almost any recipe to match your needs and tastes. It's a good idea to keep experimenting with different substitutes because it's possible to develop allergies to new foods that are eaten too frequently. Just as you were allergic to wheat, you can become allergic to barley or oats if you start eating it every day and in the same amount as the wheat.

WHEAT-FREE COOKING

Wheat and other grains—corn, rice, oats, rye, and barley—are the staples of the human diet. Because most Americans eat wheat on a daily basis, avoiding it is difficult. Wheat flour contains gluten, which helps to give a good structural framework to breads and cakes. Other flours such as rye contain little or no gluten. Regular bakeries generally combine these other flours with wheat flour to make bread. Now you can easily find gluten-free (barley, oats, wheat, and rye) baked goods at health food stores or through the internet. Because of the high demand, Whole Foods now has a bakery devoted exclusively to gluten-free bakery goods. Unfortunately, they do not have the capacity to provide allergy-free foods as well.

Baked products made without wheat flour tend to be heavier and crumble easier than those made with wheat flour. This difference is most noticeable in breads and cakes.

Oats, barley, rice, and rye can be suitable substitutions if you have a wheat allergy (see pages 76–77 for exact replacement proportions). Oats tend to produce a somewhat sticky feel in the mouth. Rice flour gives a distinct graininess to baked goods. Rye flour has a dark color and distinctive flavor. Rye baked goods are more compact and heavier than wheat products because of the low amount of gluten. Barley has a mild flavor and contains a slight amount of gluten, making it a nice substitute for wheat. Kamut is ancient wheat, and is tolerated by about 70 percent of allergic individuals. Spelt also is in the same biological family, so you will have to test each grain separately.

Because barley and other grains are closely related to wheat, some individuals are allergic to them. If you discover you have cross-reactions to other grains, you can use non-grain flour alternatives such as buckwheat, which is not a grain but a member of the rhubarb family. It makes acceptable pancakes and breads but is not a good thickener. Dark buckwheat flour, which is ground from roasted buckwheat groats, has a very strong flavor, so you might want to mix it with another non-grain flour if possible. White buckwheat flour has a mild, mellow flavor. It is made from unroasted whole groats and can be ground in a blender.

Nuts, seeds, or beans are good substitutes for anyone allergic to grains. When ground into meal, they may be substituted for any flour. Simply put one-quarter cup of nuts at a time into a blender and using on/off turns, briefly process to a fine powder. (Watch carefully; if you process too long, you'll end up with nut butter instead.)

Thickeners

Most grain flours will act as thickeners in place of wheat, but there are also several non-grain alternatives. Potato flour is useful as a thickener in sauces. When mixed with rice flour, potato flour also makes acceptable baked goods. Tapioca flour is the starch made from the fleshy root of the manioc or cassava plant. It is best used as a thickener or for small cookies.

Starchy vegetables may be used as a thickener for gravies, soups, or stews by first cooking and then mashing or pureeing. I just take a few cooked vegetables from the soup or stew and put them into a blender and puree. Then I put them back into the soup or stew. I have instant gravy.

When using alternative flours to thicken, dissolve first in cold water to prevent lumps, just as you would cornstarch. Search the internet for some of the vegetable flours, like garbanzo flour.

Noodle Substitutes

Noodles can be made from scratch using such wheat-free substitutes as amaranth flour, buckwheat flour, rice flour, or oat flour. (See Oat Noodle recipe on page 305.)

There are wheat-free noodles available through the internet or at health food stores. Eden Foods makes noodles with 100 percent buckwheat flour, for example.

Other Grain Substitutes

Amaranth is not in the grain family but in the pyrethrum family. It can be used alone as a flour substitute or mixed with grains. Amaranth was the primary source of food for the Aztecs some three thousand years ago. In order to control the Aztec population, Cortez ordered all the amaranth destroyed. It was rediscovered growing wild and is now made into a cereal or ground into flour. It is available at most health food stores.

A good substitute for those who must avoid wheat, amaranth is high in protein, and when mixed with grain or a food containing thiamine (such as pork), it provides 100 percent of the essential amino acids.

Quinoa (pronounced *keen-wa*) is similar to grains but is not in the grain family. It is in the chenopodium family, which is closely related to beets and spinach. Like amaranth, it was discovered growing in South America. Uncooked, it looks like sesame seeds. *It needs to be rinsed several times to remove the bitter protective coating.* Using a fine-meshed strainer, run cold water over the quinoa and gently rub the seeds together with your hands. Taste a few seeds; if it still has a bitter taste, continue rinsing. Quinoa cooks like rice and has a pleasant crunch. Quinoa can be used in place of any grain, in casseroles, cold salads, or desserts. It is a complete protein and contains amino acids similar to whole dried milk. Quinoa and amaranth can be easily ordered through the internet or are available at health food stores.

Wheat Substitutions

Various flours in the following quantities can be substituted for 1 cup wheat flour:

1 cup corn flour	$3/4$ cup bean flour
$3/4$ cup coarse cornmeal	1 cup barley
$3/4$ cup cornstarch	1 cup millet
$5/8$ cup potato flour	1 cup kamut
$7/8$ cup buckwheat	1 cup tapioca flour
$7/8$ cup rice flour	$1 1/4$ cups rye flour
$1 1/3$ cups ground rolled oats	$3/4$ cup potato starch
$1 1/8$ cups oat flour	$1/2$ cup ground nuts or seeds

These flour combinations are equivalent to 1 cup wheat flour:

$^1/_2$ cup rye flour + $^1/_3$ cup potato flour

$^1/_3$ cup rye flour + $^5/_8$ cup rice flour

$^5/_8$ cup rice flour + $^1/_3$ cup potato flour

$^1/_2$ cup cornstarch + $^1/_2$ cup rye flour

$^1/_2$ cup cornstarch + $^1/_2$ cup potato flour

To replace 1 tablespoon wheat flour as a thickener for sauces, gravies, and puddings, use one of the following:

$^1/_2$ tablespoon cornstarch

$^1/_2$ tablespoon potato starch

$^1/_2$ tablespoon rice flour

$^1/_2$ tablespoon arrowroot

2 teaspoons quick-cooking tapioca

2 tablespoons uncooked rice

$^1/_2$ tablespoon bean flour or nut flour

$^1/_2$ tablespoon gelatin (derived from beef and/or pork)

1 tablespoon tapioca flour

1 egg

1 teaspoon xanthan gum

Spaghetti and Noodle Substitutes (see package labels for proportions and cooking times):

- Chinese bean threads (mung beans)
- Rice
- Rice noodles
- Oat noodles
- Buckwheat noodles

Tips on Wheat-Free Cooking

- Wheat-free products should be baked at 25 degrees lower temperature and for a longer period of time.
- Some substitute flours, such as nut flours, have a higher fat content than wheat, so slightly decrease the amount of shortening in each recipe.
- When combining flours, sift several times to make sure the flours are well mixed.
- To help improve the texture of baked goods, add an extra one-half teaspoon baking power per cup of flour.
- Refrigerating dough for half an hour before baking helps improve the texture and flavor.
- Since most wheat-free baked foods will crumble, it is best to make foods with smaller surface areas, such as cupcakes instead of cakes. Use small loaf pans for quick breads. Do not pour the dough higher than two to four inches because the bottom will not cook thoroughly.
- A fast, convenient way to prepare baked goods is to buy wheat-free ready mixes by such companies as Ener-G Foods. There are many more products on the internet.

- Xanthan gum makes a great thickener in place of wheat, gelatin, or eggs. Add one teaspoon to a gluten-free recipe to hold the baked good together. It also makes a creamy smooth sauce and thickens puddings, salad dressings, and gravies. Xanthan gum can be bought at health food stores or through the internet.

CORN-FREE COOKING

Corn-derived products are probably the most difficult ingredients to eliminate completely from a diet because they are found in so many prepared foods. Because of the widespread use of corn, the best way to avoid it is by preparing your foods at home. Although corn is present in many packaged foods, you can easily cook without it.

Corn-Free Cooking Tips

- Substitute other starches, such as tapioca flour, rice flour, arrowroot, or potato starch to thicken foods.
- Use corn-free baking powder, such as Featherweight cereal-free baking powder.
- Maple syrup, maple sugar, honey, cane or beet sugar or date sugar can replace corn syrup.
- Corn-free oil such as safflower oil, canola oil, coconut oil, and sunflower oil is easy to find and just as flavorful.
- Use sea salt since regular salt contains dextrose, a corn derivative that is used to stabilize the iodine.

EGG-FREE COOKING

There are many ways to substitute eggs in a recipe, depending on what you are making. In cooking, eggs act as a binder, leavener, and thickener. If you do not use a leavening ingredient, the product will be heavier. It is best to use the following substitutes in recipes calling for one to two eggs only.

* Use an egg substitute such as Jolly Joan egg replacer. Other brands may have egg whites in them.
* Mashed bananas and apricot puree add flavor and act as both a binder and thickener in place of eggs in quick breads, cakes, cookies, or other sweets. Use two tablespoons pureed fruit for each egg called for in the recipe. Also, two tablespoons of pureed vegetables can replace an egg in soups, sauces, and other dishes.
* To bind or thicken fruit desserts, use one teaspoon dry, unflavored gelatin mixed with two tablespoons liquid to replace one egg.
* Since baked goods without eggs crumble easily, use smaller pans. For example, make cupcakes instead of a cake, or muffins instead of bread. Xanthan gum is excellent for holding baked goods together. Use 1 teaspoon per recipe.
* To help leaven a baked good, add an extra one-half teaspoon egg-free baking powder for each egg called for in a recipe along with another egg substitute to bind or thicken.
* For thickening cream dishes and sauces, add extra flour, cornstarch, or xanthan gum.
* To enhance the flavor of egg-free cookies or cakes, add extra

ingredients like butter, vanilla, raisins, nuts, coconut, seeds, or spices.
• Use egg-free mayonnaise.

MILK-FREE COOKING

Milk is difficult to avoid when buying prepared foods, but it is easy to replace in recipes. Substitute an equal amount of other liquids for milk in recipes as follows:

• Try fruits or fruit juices in place of milk on hot cereal.
• Use fruit juice, vegetable juice, pureed fruits, or pureed vegetables in place of milk in such recipes as quick breads, cookies, or cakes. Add an extra tablespoon of shortening to the recipe.
• Use goat's milk, fresh, powdered or evaporated.
• You can make a delicious banana shake. (recipe, page 115) or buy nut milk from Ener-G Foods.
• In sauces and gravies, use pure meat, chicken, or vegetable broth as a substitute for milk.
• Fry foods in safflower or another allowed oil instead of butter or margarine.
• For a great thick chocolate shake, put xanthan gum and milk substitute in a blender and mix well. Add chocolate or carob plus the allowed sweetener.
• To make sour cream, mix $1/2$ cup allowed starch with $3/4$ cup water or goat's milk, and stir in $1/4$ cup vinegar.

SUGAR-FREE COOKING

In my first edition, I used all natural sweeteners, such as honey and maple syrup. Now, these two ingredients are so expensive, I tried to cut down the sweetener as much as possible. If you can't afford honey or maple syrup you can use sugar once in a while. Eliminating foods you are allergic to is more important than eliminating sugar. In some recipes, I labeled the ingredients as "sweetener." Here you can take the liberty to use whatever type of sweetener you like.

Honey

Honey requires a little more adjustment when using in place of sugar. Use the same amount of honey as sugar or decrease by one-quarter to one-half, depending on the type of honey.

Tips on Cooking with Honey

- When baking with honey, you must account for its extra density. Each cup of honey or any syrup contains approximately $1/4$ cup of liquid. Therefore, deduct $1/4$ cup of liquid for every cup of honey or syrup being substituted.
- Add approximately $1/4$ teaspoon baking soda to whatever is called for in the recipe to neutralize the acids (all the recipes in this book have already been adjusted for you).
- Also lower the oven temperature by twenty-five degrees since honey can caramelize at a low temperature. Otherwise your baked good will become too brown on top before the inside is done.

- You can combine honey with other sweeteners for a variety in taste. Also try different brands of honey. Lighter colored honeys, such as clover, sage, and alfalfa, are milder and are good for general cooking, alone or blended.
- Buy honey from a source you can trust, as some large producers feed their bees sugar water.
- If honey crystallizes (a natural occurrence), it can be reliquefied by simply placing the container in a pan of hot water for several minutes.

Date Sugar

Date sugar is produced from ground, dried dates. It is not absorbed like regular sugar, making its use limited. For best results, use recipes specifically written for the use of date sugar. It is also good sprinkled on French toast or cereal.

Maple

Maple syrup and maple sugar can be used in place of sugar. You may want to use half the amount since it has a stronger flavor than white sugar. Decrease maple syrup proportionately as you would for honey.

Fruit Syrups

Fruit syrups can be made by boiling pure, unsweetened fruit juices (such as pear or apple) down to one-fourth or one-third of the original volume. This syrup is as sweet as maple syrup and may be substituted in equal amounts for honey or maple syrup. Also, fruit syrups are only half the cost of maple syrup or honey.

CHOCOLATE-FREE COOKING

It's rather easy to avoid chocolate in candy, cakes, frosting, ice cream, and cookies since these food products are well labeled, but you also have to watch out for cocoa, cola, and karaya gum (often listed as vegetable gum), which are closely related to chocolate.

Carob can be used as a substitute for chocolate. However, since it is in the same legume family as peas, peanuts, and soybeans, it can cause an allergic reaction.

- Substitute an equal amount of carob for chocolate.
- Oven temperatures should be lowered twenty-five degrees for baking.

6.

Children and Food Allergies

If your child is starting an allergy-free diet, you should explain the diet to him before you begin. You and he might prepare the foods together. So that your child better understands this diet and willingly participates in it, make a "contract" stating that he understands why he must be on this diet, that he is willing to stay on it, and what rewards he will earn. Create a little "reward book" in which you write down what foods he eats. Every time he eats an allergy-free meal, give him a sticker or star to place in the book. After he receives so many stickers, he earns a reward.

Make up a notebook for your child as described in chapter 2. If your child is spending a night with a friend, he and his notebook and pajamas can go off together. The friend's parents can consult the notebook to determine what foods are safe for dinner, snacks, and breakfast the next morning. They can also quickly tell which foods and ingredients to avoid.

You may also want to fill out a form similar to the one on the next page and tape it to the inside front cover of the notebook.

SCHOOL LUNCHES

Additives, preservatives, and unwanted ingredients in packaged and prepared foods can make it very difficult for a child with allergies to eat convenience foods or school lunches. To manage a diet for the allergic child at school, you may have to send along substitute foods. When your child first begins the diet, you will almost certainly have to send all foods and snacks. Make an agreement with your child that he will not trade any of his foods or eat anyone else's food (a common occurrence—trust me!).

Some schools now have systems for eliminating allergic foods from the children's school lunches. Some schools have a system where elementary school children go through a cafeteria checkout line and the child's food allergies automatically show up on a computer. The food personnel can quickly check if the child accidentally picked up any allergic foods.

Emergency Medical Information

Child's name: _____

Age:_____

Address: _____

Telephone: _____

Mother's place of work: _____

Address: _____

Telephone: _____

Father's place of work:_____

Address: _____

Telephone: _____

Physician: _____

Address: _____

City: _____State:_____Zip:_____

Telephone: _____

Hospital:_____

Address: _____

Telephone: _____

Foods to avoid (list): _____

_____

_____

Medications (include amount and times to be given):_____

_____

_____

_____

Children spend a major part of their day at school. It is important that your child and the school staff clearly understand your child's diet needs. If your child's diet permits use of some cafeteria food, ask the cafeteria worker to let your child know what foods he may have. Make a separate list of the allergic reactions your child might experience, such as a sudden earache, asthma attack, or stomach ache, and give it to the teachers.

Your child's classmates should also be told about his allergies so that they don't tempt or pressure him to eat the wrong foods. A great way to overcome other children's attitudes that your child is "different" is to go to the classroom and simply explain what allergies are. Of course, a tasty batch of homemade allergy-free cookies will convince the children that your child is actually not that different from other children.

LUNCH SUGGESTIONS

All of the following suggestions are suitable for an allergy-free diet. You'll find recipes for many of them in part 2.

- Homemade bread, rice cakes, or crackers with slices of meat or other fillings such as tuna, roast beef, pork, lamb, chicken, fish, nut butter, and homemade jelly
- Salads: chicken salad, tossed salad, turkey salad, or fruit salad
- Homemade cookies, fruit bars, cupcakes, pie, or cake (See chapters 15 and 16)
- Fruit leathers, granola (See chapter 10)
- Fruit: mixed or separate, either fresh, frozen, dried (unsulfured)

or canned (without sweetener), apples, bananas, pears, peaches, plums, nectarines, mangoes, grapes, cherries, watermelon, cantaloupe, pineapple, apricots, and strawberries
- Potato chips made with safflower oil or canola oil
- Vegetables: celery, carrots, lettuce, sliced tomatoes, cucumbers, radishes, cauliflower, mushrooms
- Individual cans or boxes of unsweetened fruit juices
- Homemade soups

Forgotten Lunches

In case your child forgets to bring a lunch to school, send a few canned food items in advance that can be stored in his locker. The school may request that the food be in sealed glass containers or cans to avoid insects.

Some suggestions for foods that can be stored at school:
- Starkist packages a 3.5-ounce serving of tuna in water with a pop-top lid. It is sold three cans to a package.
- Look for individual servings of fruits canned in their own juice or water, with a pop-top lid.
- A few brands of potato chips made with safflower oil are packaged in individual servings.
- Rice cakes can be wrapped individually and kept a long time. They contain no preservatives or additives.
- Nuts and seeds without additives or preservatives can be bought in small individual packages.
- Small individual cans or paper cartons of unsweetened juice will store a long time.

Tips for preparing lunches

- Put together a week's worth of sandwiches at a time. Spread each slice of bread with a very thin layer of butter, mayonnaise, or margarine. This will prevent the bread from becoming soggy. Add the meat or spread, wrap, label, and freeze. Take the sandwich out in the morning and it will thaw before lunch. Put lettuce and tomato in a separate bag.
- Use healthy oatmeal bread (see page 130) or hardy store bought bread that is more substantial.
- Package and freeze small quantities of meat, poultry, or spread and put packages into the lunch box at the last minute.
- Freeze individual cartons or boxes of pure fruit juice. They will thaw out but still be cold by lunchtime. (Before packing frozen juice into a paper bag, put it in a separate plastic bag. Otherwise moisture on the outside of the juice container may cause the bag to rip.)
- If possible, make lunch the night before to avoid early morning hassles. Right after dinner is a great time to pack lunch. Put leftovers in small containers and refrigerate or freeze immediately.

EATING AWAY FROM HOME

Before you and your child go to a restaurant, plan ahead. Most restaurants do not offer specialized allergy-free menus. At most fine restaurants knowledgeable chefs can cater to your family's individual needs. Remember that the same dish at two different restaurants may have different ingredients. Always ask before you order anything.

National chain restaurants generally use the same type of ingredients throughout their restaurants. Inquire about the foods at these various chain restaurants so that you will know which ones are acceptable. If eating out at a restaurant or other social gathering is awkward for you because you are worried about your child eating something he is allergic to, call up the restaurant in advance to see if they can accommodate your child's needs.

Traveling by Car

An overnight stay might require bringing along whatever foods are necessary. Traveling by car can be enjoyable for your family if you plan ahead and have the room to take along enough canned and refrigerated foods. Even if you plan to eat at restaurants while you travel, you may still need to bring along additional foods. Restaurants would rather have you bring your own foods to substitute than see your child have a reaction to the food from their restaurant.

When my daughter was around six years old, she would fly from South Bend to Chicago by herself to visit her grandparents. At that time, all I had available was fresh raw goat's milk that I got from the local farmer. I would pack the milk in ice. I'd walk my daughter to the commercial plane and hand the container of milk to the pilot to safely store away. My, have times changed!

Below are some suggested foods that you might take along when you travel while you or your children are on an allergy-free diet:
- Rye crackers, such as natural Ry-Krisp (it contains just rye)
- Small cans of unsweetened fruit juices

- Nut butters (if allowed)
- Seeds and nuts (if allowed)
- Fruit, either fresh or canned in its own juice, such as unsweetened applesauce or pineapple
- Milk substitute, such as evaporated or powdered goat's milk, or nut milk (if tolerated)
- Dried fruits (Some dried fruits are preserved with sulfur, so check the label. Honey-coated fruits may also have been treated with other preservatives. Dark raisins are sun dried, without preservatives, whereas golden light raisins are preserved with sulfur.)
- Sweeteners, pure maple sugar granules (which come in a small plastic shaker)
- Homemade muffins and breads
- Fresh vegetables
- Plain canned fish or meat, such as tuna packed in water or chicken in water, not chicken broth (read the ingredients carefully)

Traveling by Plane

If your child has food allergies, you may find it more satisfactory to bring his own meals with him and to plan on eating beforehand. Just pack his foods and snacks in his lunch box or backpack. That way he can eat whatever and whenever he wants. It's best to have extra meals in case of delays or cancellations, something that happens quite frequently now.

FOOD ALLERGIES AND HOLIDAYS

Birthdays

Putting together a birthday party for a child with food allergies requires some extra planning. Although traditional birthday and holiday foods are allergen-containing, you can make delicious allergy-free substitutes so that your child can enjoy a special occasion without suffering a food reaction. (Remember, it's crucial to maintain the diet at all times, especially during holidays and special occasions.)

If your child wants traditional cake and ice cream, that's fine. Just make the cake yourself (see chapter 16 for recipes) or find a baker who will follow your recipe. Perhaps a friend will make an allergen-free cake for the child as a present.

Many cakes made without wheat flour or eggs crumbly easily. Don't try a two-layer cake. The batter will produce great cupcakes that can be individually decorated. Or you can make cupcakes for everyone, using a regular recipe for the guests and an allergy-free recipe for your child. Just try the recipes ahead of time before the actual party. You might discover you have to adjust the recipe. Recently, I have seen bakeries arrange cupcakes into a unique shape for parties on Valentine's Day, graduation day, or a birthday. They heavily frost the cupcakes, so you don't see the shape of the cupcake; and you simply pull apart the cupcakes at the party. The bakery can add all kinds of other decorations or pictures on it. If you are not allergic to the frosting, you could have the bakery make allergy-free cupcakes for your child.

The first time I tested one of my muffin recipes I was developing for this cookbook, they turned into bouncing beige balls—not muffins.

And of course that was the day the reporter came to interview me about writing my book. I *never* would have told her about my failures. But, of course, that was also the day my daughter was home sick from school. She told the reporter *everything* about how fantastic my bouncing muffins were. Of course, my professionalism and devotion to writing the cookbook were overlooked, and the bouncing muffins made the front page!

I received so many phone calls with suggestions to sell the patent to a toy company or people wondering if you can turn your muffin into a slinky. So, try all your recipes first. Once you get cupcakes you like, you can freeze them, with or without frosting. It's one less step before the party. But you *must* try out all recipes before any kind of special gathering or event; it could save you a lot of disappointment when company comes.

Easter

Traditional Easter goodies—colored eggs, chocolate bunnies, and jelly beans—may have to be avoided by children with food allergies. Parents can help their allergic children celebrate a traditional Easter by being inventive. Substitute plastic eggs filled with small trinkets such as balloons, coins, or jewelry. If the child is allergic to the plastic, make a paper ball. Cut colorful crepe paper into thin strips and wrap the paper around small trinkets. Continue adding trinkets and wrapping the paper around them until you have a large ball.

So that your child won't miss out on decorating Easter eggs, take a raw egg and puncture each end with a needle. Blow out the egg and rinse the inside of the shell a few times, then decorate with markers, paints, and crayons. If your child is severely allergic to eggs, you can buy plastic eggs and paint them. Make tasty Easter surprises out of maple sugar or make cookies in the shape of bunnies or eggs.

Halloween

Since Halloween involves leaving home to go trick-or-treating, it presents special problems. Tell your neighbors about your children's allergies and ask them if they could provide something suitable for your child. Either a snack (such as fruit or allergen-free cookies) or small trinkets such as pencils, balloons, or money would delight any child.

Another possibility, have a Halloween party at home so you can plan for children with food allergies and provide safe allergy-free foods.

Christmas

For most people, the days between Thanksgiving and the New Year are filled with family get-togethers and holiday party celebrations. Although this can be a difficult time for the person with food allergies, careful planning and preparation can free you from unexpected allergic reactions. Here are a few suggestions to help you during this busy time of the year:

- Plan your holiday menus well in advance.
- Order special ingredients early.
- Prepare as much food ahead of time as possible and freeze. Cookies, breads, and cakes freeze well and thaw rapidly if unexpected company arrives. Have a few meals frozen and ready to heat for overwhelmingly hectic days.
- Make foods that are suitable for entertaining, such as Oatmeal

Bread, Pecan Balls, or Carob Candy. (See pages 130, 256, and 269).

Children suffer from an occasional illness for which your physician might prescribe a soft or liquid diet. Generally, soft diets consist of puddings, soups, and ice cream, while a liquid diet restricts intakes to gelatins, carbonated beverages, juices, and broths.

During an illness, an individual's allergic threshold is often lowered. Food preparation then becomes increasingly important. Not only must the child's nutritional needs be met, but also adequate fluid intake (hydration) must be maintained.

The following is a listing of allergen-free substitutes/alternatives for foods commonly taken as part of a liquid or soft diet. Recipes will be found in part 2.

- For carbonated beverages, substitute pure fruit juices and carbonated water, or mixed fruit juices.
- For ice cream and popsicles, substitute homemade sherbets, popsicles and ice creams, frozen fruits, and juices.
- For packaged puddings and gelatin desserts, substitute homemade puddings and gelatin desserts, applesauce, and pureed fruits.
- For soups and cereals, substitute homemade broths, cream of rice, and cream of buckwheat.

When my children were young, I always had a box set aside which contained a few bottles of juice, carbonated water, Pedialyte (the plain, unflavored type), small containers of applesauce, sugar-free and dye-free fruit gelatin mixes, Cream of Rice, medicine, toys, activities, and a Tupperware popsicle maker. I could easily make ice cream, popsicles, or pudding if they wanted since I'd mix all the dry ingredients ahead of time for the gelatin and pudding. I also had a twenty-minute ice cream maker—I keep the mixer in the freezer all the time, then simply add the ingredients and mix it for twenty minutes; no ice is necessary.

Since we lived far out in the country, it was not practical to run to town when my kids got sick. Also the stores might be closed or the product might be hard to find.

By planning ahead for all of your children's special dietary needs, you will alleviate many of your worries and know that wherever your child is, he will be safe and stay as healthy as possible.

Part Two

RECIPES

7.

Meal Planning and Menus

All of the recipes in this section exclude most or all of the major eight allergens: milk, egg, wheat, soybeans, peanuts, tree nuts, fish, and shellfish. In addition, other common allergens are excluded: chilies, chili pepper, garlic, onion, cinnamon, and coffee, plus additives, preservatives, and colorings. Once you have tested these foods and know which ones you are allergic to, you can use these same recipes and add the ingredients that do not produce allergic reactions. Many of the recipes have suggestions for adding back foods. You will also find recipes that eliminate some, but not all, of these allergens. Most of these can also be modified for your particular allergies. For appropriate substitutions and equivalent measures, see chapter 5.

TIMESAVING TECHNIQUES

To save time, make breads, muffins, pancakes, cookies, and "TV dinners" in advance of serving. Divide the foods into individual or meal-size portions and wrap with aluminum foil. Then put into a gallon freezer bag. Label, date, and freeze.

If you are freezing a casserole, line the baking dish with aluminum foil and pour in the casserole. Cover the casserole dish with a sheet of foil and fold the edges together, sealing tightly and pressing the air out. Label, date, and freeze. When frozen solid, lift from the pan, put into a gallon freezer bag, and return the frozen package to the freezer. To serve, preheat the oven to approximately 425°F and place the foil package in its original pan. Bake, covered, for approximately thirty-five minutes. Remove the top sheet of foil and bake an additional ten to fifteen minutes, until the sauce is hot and bubbly.

If the casserole includes meat, precooking the meat will eliminate greasiness and shorten the reheating time.

When reheating individual portions in a microwave, remove the foil and put the food on a microwave-safe plate. Cover with plastic wrap, turning back one edge to vent. Microwave on high power for four to seven minutes, or until thoroughly heated.

Since you will need to spend more time in the kitchen preparing special allergy-free foods, try to prepare a few meals at one time. For example, prepare double the amount of food you need for a meal and freeze the remainder. When planning your menus, create meals in which you can use the same foods. For example, when coring apples for fresh applesauce at breakfast or lunch, core extra apples for an Apple Crisp dessert. When shredding potatoes for hash browns, shred extra for Potato Pancakes. Store the potatoes in water with a small amount of ascorbic acid (vitamin C).

While in the kitchen preparing your regular meal, make a sauce or soup that needs to simmer for a long time. For example, spaghetti sauce takes only a few minutes to mix together but needs to simmer for a few hours. If you want to use hamburger in the sauce, plan a casserole or dish for your evening meal that uses browned hamburger. Brown the hamburger for both meals and divide it for the casserole and spaghetti sauce.

An electric slow cooker is a great time-saver. Just before bedtime, add whole grains and the necessary water and cook all night on low. Breakfast will be ready to eat in the morning. Or cook some meat for breakfast. After breakfast, place some vegetables on top of the meat and let them simmer until lunch or dinner. You can also make soup, chili, or beef stew and have it ready to eat any time of the day.

Set aside one day a week or so and prepare the basic "staples" for your diet. For example, make oat noodles first (this allows time for the noodles to dry before freezing), and then mix up granola (the grain needs to be heated). Make up several loaves of bread, slice, wrap each piece individually (or place waxed paper between the slices), and freeze. You can also mix the dry ingredients together for pancakes, muffins, or biscuits. Later all you have to do is add the liquid and cook.

Freeze nuts in their shells or remove the shells to save space in the freezer. Frozen nuts can last for approximately three to six months if well-wrapped.

When grinding nuts and seeds or shredding coconut, prepare a large amount (such as four to six cups). Buy large amounts of fruits at one time, such as bananas or apples, and eat them as they ripen. When the apples will no longer keep, peel, slice, and puree in a blender or food processor and freeze in half-pint containers. Packed in a lunch box, the apple puree will thaw out by noon. If you like, you can add chopped nuts, seeds, coconut, or dried fruit to the pureed fruit. If you have extra bananas, peel and freeze some of them whole. When frozen, you can roll them in chopped nuts or make the recipe for Frosty Freezer Treats (see page 262). My kids loved making that because it was so messy!

MENUS

In developing the menu suggestions for the allergy-free diet, I have put together foods that complement one another in flavor and in nutritional value. All of the menus are more than you will eat, but I have provided them simply to give you ideas.

Breakfast

TIP: Make Oatmeal Bread ahead of time, slice, wrap separately, and freeze.

Toasted Oatmeal Bread* with
Strawberry Jam* and Nut Butter*

Hot Cocoa made with nut milk*

Banana-Pineapple Cooler*

TIP: Grate potatoes the night before and store in a container filled with water and ascorbic acid to prevent them from turning dark.

Fresh Homemade Applesauce*

Potato Pancakes*

Pure pork sausage

Apple Oatmeal*

Turkey burgers

TIP: Use fresh ground turkey and add your own allowed seasonings, as the turkey tastes very bland.

Grape juice

Fresh cantaloupe

Apple Rice Betty*

Nut Milk

Sliced fresh peaches

TIP: Squeeze pineapple juice onto the peaches to keep them from turning brown.

Oat Muffins*

TIP: Freeze extra ripe bananas to make frosty beverages that can have the consistency of soft ice cream.

Banana Shake

Fresh sliced fruit

Amaranth Granola

Pork patties

Cantaloupe and watermelon balls

Apple Spice Oatmeal

Crunchy Granola*

---

* RECIPES INCLUDED.

Lunch

TIP: Cook fresh turkey; do not use packaged lunch meat.

Tropical Shake*

Homemade Tomato Soup*

Carrot Bread* with sliced turkey

Pecan Balls*

Banana Shake*

Chicken Soup*

Oatmeal Crackers*

Tuna Salad Luau*

Carob Candy*

Chicken and Potato Soup*

Broiled Burgers*

Catsup*

Potato chips

TIP: Buy potato chips processed with canola or safflower oil.

Applesauce*

Spaghetti sauce served over Spaghetti Squash

Stuffed Mushrooms*

Sunflower Salad*

Raisin Nut Cookies*

TIP: Double the batch of spaghetti sauce and freeze extra.

Also double the stuffed mushrooms as they freeze well too.

TIP: The soup tastes better after a day or so.

Minestrone Soup*

Carrot and celery sticks

Molded Fruit Gelatin*

Rice-Flour Biscuits*

Pea Soup

Banana Honey Salad*

Radishes

TIP: RyKrisp bought at the supermarket can be substituted for the recipe Rye Crisp; but be sure to read the label— there are several types.

Rye Crisps*

*RECIPES INCLUDED.

Dinner

Fruit Melon Shake*

TIP: The Pork Chop Spanish Rice freezes well. Pork Chop Spanish Rice*

Braised Celery*

Molded Fruit Gelatin*

Almond Crescents*

Chicken or Turkey Loaf*

Mashed potatoes

Eggplant with Tomato*

Biscuits*

TIP: Mix all the dry ingredients together for the biscuits and cut in the shortening. Store in the refrigerator until ready to bake, then add the liquid.

Pineapple Pork Chops with Rice*

Tossed salad with French Dressing*

Green Beans

TIP: I always keep French dressing ready in the refrigerator.

Fruity Spice Cake*

Quick Savory Meat Loaf*

TIP: The meat loaf freezes well.

Baked potato

Maple Carrots*

Cranberry Relish*

Watermelon Sherbet*

Baked Turkey Breast or Leg

Baked Sweet Potatoes*

Cranberry Relish*

Pumpkin Pecan Pie*

TIP: You don't have to wait until Thanksgiving to enjoy these delicious flavors

---

Chicken Supreme with Mushroom Sauce*

Oriental Tomato Skillet*

Green Beans with Almonds*

Banana Cake*

Fried fish with Tartar Sauce*

Confetti Rice*

Tossed salad with oil and vinegar

Pumpkin Pecan Pie*

TIP: Wrap extra cooked Chicken Supreme with sauce in individual portions and freeze, or make up "TV dinners." All these foods freeze well. Great for those really hectic days.

TIP: Make up your own dressing of oil and add your favorite allowed vinegar and seasonings.

Chicken Broth or Soup*

Hearty Lamb Pilaf*

Strawberry Pie*

TIP: Freeze extra soup in ice cube trays and store in a plastic bag. Take out several cubes and heat for a cup of soup.

*RECIPES INCLUDED.

SLOW COOKER COOKING

Now, if you have no time at all to cook, here is what I did when I had to work very, very long hours. I used the slow cooker (two, in fact), a breadmaker, and a food processor to cut all the vegetables.

Each night, my three-quart slow cooker cooked a different grain or substitute (buckwheat and tapioca aren't grains), and I'd eat that in the morning. If I needed rice for my evening meal, I'd begin cooking that in the morning.

I'd prepare my meals the night before and put the lining of the slow cooker in the refrigerator. I'd start cooking it in the morning. It would be wonderful walking into my home, smelling the aroma of the foods. I usually could sit down and eat right away when I worked a long day. (I planned it that way.) On days when I got home earlier, I used up the leftovers and made such things as chicken soup, Alfredo primavera, chicken or beef stir-fry, or lasagna.

For lunch I sometimes ate leftovers from the night before. Usually I had some fruit and/or a vegetable salad. I made the salad when I cut up the vegetables for dinner.

I also used a lot of precut fruits and vegetables that I got from the salad bar at the supermarket; I just made sure they were preservative-free. When I worked outside the home, I had a routine like this:

Sunday Night
- Cooked hamburger and added to slow cooker (6 quart)
- Added all ingredients for spaghetti sauce
- Froze chicken pieces for dinner on Tuesday

Monday Morning

- Ate "Spaghetti Sauce"; tastes like tomato vegetable soup, allowed it to continue to cook on low
- Mixed up bread in bread maker, to be ready at night

Monday Evening

- Put spaghetti squash in oven; enjoyed spaghetti dinner with thick spaghetti sauce over squash and fresh baked bread

Monday Night

- Mixed up steel cut oatmeal to be ready for Tuesday morning (3-quart slow cooker)
- Sliced and stirred strawberries and other ingredients for fresh jam in breadmaker
- Put water and seasonings, vegetables, and potatoes into slow cooker (6 quart) and refrigerated.

Tuesday Morning

- Added frozen chicken pieces to vegetable mixture; and turned on low for 10 to 12 hours or high for $4\frac{1}{2}$ to $5\frac{1}{2}$ hours
- Had oatmeal with dollop of fresh strawberries and cream
- Made rice in 3-quart slow cooker

Tuesday Evening

- Mixed up bread ingredients for bread and put in bread machine; set to bake for morning
- Enjoyed chicken with potatoes and vegetables

Wednesday Morning
- For breakfast, ate fresh bread with butter and jam

Wednesday Evening
- Made lasagna dinner with leftover spaghetti sauce
- Enjoyed fresh salad

Thursday Evening
- Made Alfredo primavera using broth, leftover chicken, mushroom, and parmesan
- Put pot roast in with potatoes and vegetables in slow cooker and refrigerated

Friday Morning
- Cooked pot roast (6-quart slow cooker)
- Made bread pudding with leftover bread for dessert

Friday Evening
- Enjoyed delightful pot roast dinner

8.

Beverages

Living without cow's milk seems to be one of the most difficult adjustments an allergic individual must deal with. In our research kitchen we have developed an exciting and unusual array of great tasting beverages. You'll hardly notice the absence of a glass of milk at mealtime. Just don't forget to take your calcium supplement, preferably with added vitamins D and K.

APRICOT-APPLE SHAKE . . .113

BANANA-PEACH DRINK . . .114

BANANA-PINEAPPLE COOLER . . .113

BANANA SHAKE . . .115

CARROT MILK . . .116

COCONUT MILK . . .116

FRESH APPLE COOLER . . .117

FRESH MELON SHAKE . . .117

FRUIT SLUSH . . .118

HOT COCOA . . .119

KIWIFRUIT SPRITZER . . .120

LEMONADE . . .121

TOMATO JUICE COCKTAIL . . .122

TROPICAL SHAKE . . .123

Apricot-Apple Shake

1 (16-ounce) can water-packed red apricots, drained

$^1/_2$ cup applesauce

$^1/_2$ cup nut milk or goat's milk

6 to 10 ice cubes

Combine all the ingredients in a blender and liquefy.

Makes 2$^3/_4$ cups

VARIATIONS, IF TOLERATED:
- Substitute an equal amount of milk for the milk substitute.

Banana-Pineapple Cooler

2 cups cold pineapple juice

5 to 6 pineapple chunks

2 ripe bananas, cut into pieces

Pour the pineapple juice into the container of a blender and, at high speed, add the chunks of fruit a few at a time. Blend until smooth and frothy.

Makes 3 cups

Banana-Peach Drink

2 very ripe bananas, cut into pieces

2 very ripe peaches, peeled and sliced

1 cup juice, goat's milk, or milk substitute

$1/4$ cup sugar

2 teaspoons lemon juice

Mint leaves (optional)

Freeze banana slices and peaches until very firm, except save a few slices for garnish. When fruits are frozen, place in a blender with the milk, sugar, and lemon juice. Blend at high speed, pushing the fruit down carefully, until the mixture is blended and has the consistency of soft ice cream. Garnish with fresh mint leaves and fruit slices, if desired. Serve immediately.

Makes 2 cups

Banana Shake

2 cups cold water

$1/3$ cup raw cashews (optional)

1 or 2 large frozen bananas, cut into pieces

1 tablespoon honey

$1/2$ teaspoon vanilla

Pour the water into the container of a blender. If using cashews, add them and process on high to make a nut milk. Add the bananas a few pieces at a time and blend until smooth. Add the other ingredients and blend to mix thoroughly. Serve immediately.

Makes 3 cups

> Hint: To freeze the bananas, peel, and wrap In a Ziploc freezer bag and freeze until solid.

VARIATIONS, IF TOLERATED:
- Substitute an equal amount of milk for the water.
- Substitute an equal amount of sugar for the honey.
- Add 2 fresh ripe peaches in place of the bananas.

Carrot Milk

This is an excellent drink for children.

2 cups milk or milk substitute

3 medium carrots, cut into 1-inch pieces

Put ingredients in blender container; cover and run on high until carrots are liquefied.

Makes 4 servings

Coconut Milk

Meat of 1 fresh coconut, cut into pieces

Liquid from 1 fresh coconut

2 cups hot water

Whirl all the ingredients in a blender at high speed until liquefied. Strain in a sieve, pressing out the liquid. The milk can by used in recipes and freezes well. (Use the coconut left in the sieve for baking.)

Makes 2 cups

Fresh Apple Cooler

$^1/_2$ cup water

1 tablespoon lemon juice

1 teaspoon sugar

1 apple, peeled, cored and cut into 1-inch cubes

$^1/_2$ cup ice, crushed

Put all ingredients except ice in blender container; cover and run on high until apple is liquefied. Add crushed ice; cover and run on high until ice is liquefied. Taste and add 1–2 additional teaspoons sugar, if necessary.

Makes 2 servings

Fresh Melon Shake

$^1/_2$ cup pineapple juice

2 cups ripe melon, cubed

Pour the juice into the container of a blender and, at high speed, add the cubed fruit a few pieces at a time. Blend thoroughly, adding more melon if a thicker shake is desired.

Makes 2$^1/_2$ cups

Fruit Slush

2 cups water, juice, or milk

$1/2$ cup fresh pineapple chunks

$1/2$ cup strawberries, frozen

Sweetener to taste

Blend the ingredients together until mixed well. Serve immediately.

Makes 3 cups

> **Hint:** To prepare frozen strawberries, wash the strawberries and remove their stems. Arrange the strawberries on a cookie sheet and place in the freezer. Freeze until solid (1 to 2 hours). If not using the strawberries right away, put them in a plastic freezer bag.

Hot Cocoa

With the creation of hot cocoa mixes, most people have forgotten how to make hot cocoa from "scratch." I've added this recipe so you can make any type of hot cocoa you want; use carob or cocoa, use sugar or honey, use milk or nut milk. It's all up to you.

$1/4$ cup cocoa or carob

$1/4$ cup sugar or other sweetener

$1/4$ teaspoon sea salt

1 cup hot water

3 cups milk or substitute, scalded

1 teaspoon vanilla

In a medium-size saucepan, stir together the cocoa and sugar and salt. If there are a lot of lumps, you might want to sift it.

Slowly add the water and milk or milk substitute, heating just until it comes to a boil. Add the vanilla and serve immediately.

Makes 4 servings

Kiwifruit Spritzer

3 kiwifruit, peeled

2 tablespoons sugar or other sweetener

$1/2$ cup orange juice

$1 1/2$ cups club soda

Kiwifruit slices, lemon wedges or mint as garnish (optional)

Ice as needed

Combine the kiwifruit, sugar, and orange juice in a blender. Whirl until smooth. Pour $1/2$ cup into a tall (12-ounce) glass. Add ice and pour in $1/2$ cup club soda. Stir to combine. Garnish with kiwifruit slices, lemon wedges, or mint, if desired. Serve immediately.

Makes 3 spritzers

Lemonade

$1/2$ cup lemon juice, fresh (no substitute)*

$1/2$ cup sugar or sugar substitute

2 cups ice, crushed

Put all ingredients in blender container; cover and run on high about 10 seconds. Pour into 4 tall glasses and fill with water.

Makes 4 servings

*Note:** Bottled lemon juice contains sulfite.

VARIATIONS, IF TOLERATED, FOR PINK LEMONADE:
- Add $3/4$ cup sweet cherry juice or $3/4$ cup frozen strawberries to ingredients before blending; blend until smooth.

Tomato Juice Cocktail

1 $\frac{1}{2}$ cups tomato juice

$\frac{1}{2}$ cup evaporated goat's milk or milk substitute

$\frac{1}{4}$ teaspoon celery salt

$\frac{1}{4}$ teaspoon sea salt

$\frac{1}{2}$ cup ice, crushed

Put all ingredients in blender; cover and run on high until smooth and frothy.

Makes 4 servings

Tropical Shake

1 banana, frozen

$1/2$ cup unsweetened coconut

2 tablespoons nut butter

$2^1/2$ cups nut milk or other milk substitute

$1/2$ teaspoon pure vanilla

Puree the banana, coconut, nut butter, and 1 cup of the nut milk or allowed substitute. Blend until creamy, then add the remaining nut milk and vanilla.

Makes 4 cups

VARIATIONS, IF TOLERATED:
- Substitute an equal amount of milk for the milk substitute.

9.

Breads, Muffins, Biscuits, and Crackers

For the person who has food allergies, especially to milk, eggs, and wheat, finding acceptable breads can be a major problem.

Try these recipes first, and once you have gained some experience in allergy-free cooking, create your own favorites. Don't be afraid to use new ingredients such as oats, amaranth, xanthan gum, tapioca starch, or buckwheat.

QUICK BREADS

APRICOT ALMOND BREAD ...127

BANANA BREAD ...128

CARROT BREAD ...129

OATMEAL BREAD ...130

STREUSEL-TOPPED COFFEE CAKE ...131

ZUCCHINI NUT BREAD ...132

YEAST BREADS

PUMPERNICKEL BREAD ...133

RICE FLOUR BREAD ...134

MUFFINS

BLUEBERRY OAT MUFFINS ...136

CORN MUFFINS ...137

NUT BUTTER RICE MUFFINS ...138

OAT MUFFINS ...139

RAISIN MUFFINS ...139

NUT MUFFINS ...139

BANANA OAT MUFFINS ...139

RICE FLOUR MUFFINS ...140

BISCUITS AND CRACKERS

ALMOND BISCUITS ...141

DRIED CHERRY SPELT SCONES ...142

RICE FLOUR BISCUITS ...143

SCOTTISH OATCAKES ...144

OATMEAL CRACKERS ...145

RYE CRISPS ...146

Apricot Almond Bread

1 $^3/_4$ cups dried apricots, unsulfured

$^1/_4$ cup butter or margarine

1 $^1/_2$ cups sugar

2 cups wheat flour

2 teaspoons baking powder

$^1/_2$ teaspoon baking soda

$^1/_2$ teaspoon sea salt

$^2/_3$ cup coconut milk or water

$^1/_2$ cup almonds, chopped

Preheat the oven to 350°F. Grease a 9 x 5-inch loaf pan.

In a small saucepan, add enough water to cover the apricots and simmer for 5 minutes. Drain the fruit and reserve the juice. Chop the apricots. Cream the butter and sugar and stir in $^1/_2$ cup of the reserved apricot juice. Combine the flour with the baking powder, baking soda, and salt. Stir the dry ingredients into the creamed mixture alternately with coconut milk, stirring the batter only until combined. Fold in the almonds. Pour the batter into the loaf pan and bake for 1 hour, or until done.

Makes 1 loaf

VARIATIONS, IF TOLERATED:
- Substitute an equal amount of milk for the coconut milk or water.

Banana Bread

$^2/_3$ cup oil

1 cup sugar

2 eggs

1 $^1/_2$ cups ripe bananas, mashed

1 teaspoon vanilla

1 $^3/_4$ cups barley or wheat flour

1 teaspoon sea salt

1 teaspoon baking soda

1 cup walnuts (optional)

Preheat the oven to 325°F. Grease a 9 x 5-inch or 8 $^1/_2$ x 4 $^1/_2$-inch (for a taller loaf) loaf pan.

In a large bowl, mix the oil and sugar. Add the eggs one at a time, beating well after each addition. Blend in the bananas and vanilla. Mix together the flour, salt, and baking soda and stir into the banana mixture. Add the nuts if desired. Pour into a loaf pan and bake for approximately 1 hour, or until done. Remove from the pan and cool on a wire rack.

Makes 1 loaf

Carrot Bread

1 cup raw carrots, shredded

$^3/_4$ cup maple syrup or maple sugar or sugar

$^1/_2$ cup safflower oil

1 $^1/_2$ cups oat flour

1 teaspoon baking soda

2 teaspoons baking powder

1 teaspoon nutmeg (optional)

$^1/_2$ teaspoon sea salt

$^1/_2$ cup raisins

$^1/_4$ cup chopped walnuts (optional)

Preheat the oven to 350°F. Grease the bottom of a 9 x 5-inch or 8 x 4-inch loaf pan.

In a large bowl, combine the carrots, syrup, and oil. Stir for 1 minute. In a smaller bowl, add the dry ingredients and blend. Add to the carrot mixture and stir until just combined. Mix in the raisins and nuts and pour into the loaf pan. Bake for 1 hour, or until a tester inserted in the center comes out clean. Remove from the pan and cool completely.

Makes 1 loaf

VARIATIONS, IF TOLERATED:
- Add 1 egg along with the syrup and oil.
- Substitute 2 cups of wheat for the oat flour.

Oatmeal Bread

This delicious bread is great for making sandwiches.

1 cup rolled oats

1 cup hot water

$1/4$ to $1/2$ cup maple syrup or honey

$1/4$ teaspoon sea salt

1 banana, mashed

1 cup oat flour

$1/4$ teaspoon baking soda

3 teaspoons baking powder

Preheat the oven to 350°F. Grease a 9 x 5-inch loaf pan.

Mix the rolled oats with the hot water. Let stand for 5 minutes. Stir in the honey, salt, and banana. Mix the dry ingredients together. Add to the banana-oat mixture and stir until all the ingredients are just mixed. Do not overmix. Turn into the loaf pan and let stand for 20 minutes in a warm place. Bake for 45 minutes.

Makes 1 loaf

VARIATIONS, IF TOLERATED:
- Substitute an equal amount of sugar for the honey.
- Add 2 eggs in place of or in addition to the mashed banana.
- Add $1/2$ cup chopped nuts or raisins.

Streusel-Topped Coffee Cake

2 cups oat flour

$^1/_3$ cup sugar

3 teaspoons baking powder

$^1/_2$ teaspoon sea salt

$^1/_4$ cup butter or margarine, softened

2 eggs

$^1/_2$ to $^2/_3$ cup milk, nut milk, or goat's milk

TOPPING

$^1/_4$ cup packed brown sugar OR $^1/_8$ cup honey or maple syrup

1 teaspoon nutmeg (optional)

$^1/_4$ cup chopped nuts (optional)

1 tablespoon butter or margarine, melted

Preheat the oven to 375°F. Lightly grease an 8-inch square pan.

Mix together the oat flour, sugar, baking powder, and salt. Add the butter, eggs, and milk. Beat until smooth. Pour the batter into the pan. Mix the topping ingredients together and sprinkle onto the batter. Bake for 30 to 35 minutes.

Makes 6 servings

Zucchini Nut Bread

3 eggs

$^3/_4$ cup oil

1 cup honey

2 cups grated and tightly packed zucchini

3 cups barley or wheat flour

2 teaspoons baking powder

$^1/_2$ teaspoon baking soda

$^1/_2$ teaspoon sea salt

1 $^1/_2$ teaspoons nutmeg (optional)

$^1/_2$ teaspoon ground ginger

1 $^1/_2$ teaspoons vanilla

1 cup chopped nuts (optional)

Preheat the oven to 350°F. Grease three 7$^1/_2$ x 3$^1/_2$-inch or two 9 x 5-inch loaf pans and dust with barley flour. Shake out the excess flour.

Beat the eggs in a large mixing bowl. Stir in the oil and honey, then the zucchini. Combine the dry ingredients and add to the bowl. Gently stir in the vanilla and nuts. Pour the batter into loaf pans. Bake for 50 to 55 minutes, or until done. Let stand a few minutes, then turn onto a wire rack to cool. Wrapped tightly, the bread freezes well.

Makes 2 or 3 loaves

VARIATIONS, IF TOLERATED:
- **Substitute an equal amount of sugar for the honey.**

Pumpernickel Bread

Of German origin, this recipe makes a firm dark bread. Because rye has little gluten, it will not rise as much as bread made from wheat flour.

6 cups rye flour

1 tablespoon sea salt

$1/4$ cup butter or margarine

2 tablespoons honey

$1^3/4$ cups milk, nut milk, or goat's milk

1 package dry yeast

$2/3$ cup tepid water

1 tablespoon caraway seeds

Preheat the oven to 400°F. Lightly grease two 9 x 5-inch loaf pans or a cookie sheet.

In a large bowl, mix the rye flour and salt. Cut the butter or margarine into small pieces and cut into the flour. In a small saucepan, combine the honey and milk. Cook over very low heat until the honey has dissolved and the milk is lukewarm. Combine the yeast and water and mix until the yeast is dissolved. Make a well in the flour mixture and pour in the yeast liquid and the warm milk and honey. Mix until a sticky dough has formed.

Turn the dough out onto a floured surface and knead it well for 10 minutes, or until the dough is firm and no longer sticky. Add more flour if necessary. Put the dough into a lightly greased bowl and cover with greased plastic wrap, or put it into a large greased plastic bag. Allow the dough to rise in a warm place for 45 to 60 minutes, or until it has doubled in bulk.

When the dough has risen, turn it out onto a lightly floured surface and knead it again for 2 to 3 minutes. Divide the dough in half, shape it into two ovals, and put them on a lightly greased baking sheet or into two loaf pans. Sprinkle caraway seeds over the loaves and press the seeds into the dough. Cover the dough and put in a warm place to rise until doubled in bulk or raised to the top of the pans. Bake for 45 minutes, or until the loaves are dark brown and sound hollow when tapped underneath. Cool on a wire rack.

Makes 2 loaves

Rice Flour Bread

2^1/$_4$ cups warm water

4^1/$_2$ teaspoons dry yeast

^{1}/$_4$ cup honey

4^1/$_4$ cups brown rice flour

^{1}/$_2$ cup sunflower seeds, ground

1 carrot, grated

4^1/$_2$ teaspoons xanthan gum

1 teaspoon nutmeg

1 teaspoon dried herbs or lemon rind, grated

^{1}/$_3$ cup oil

2 eggs (optional)

2 to 4 tablespoons sesame seeds

Preheat the oven to 200°F. Grease two 8 x 4-inch loaf pans.

Combine the water, yeast, and honey in a cup. Set aside for 10 minutes, until the yeast is foamy. Place the flour in a large bowl in a 200°F oven for 10 to 15 minutes to warm it. (Then preheat the oven to 400°F.) Remove 1 cup of the flour and reserve. To the remaining flour add the sunflower seeds, carrot, xanthan gum, nutmeg, and dried herbs. Mix well.

Make a well in the center of the flour and add the oil, eggs, and the yeast mixture. Using an electric mixer, beat at high speed for 3 minutes. Stop and scrape the sides of the bowl. Add the reserved flour. Beat at low speed for 1 minute. Scrape the batter off the beaters and level the surface of the dough. Oil the top of the dough and the sides of the bowl above the dough. Cover the bowl with a damp towel. Place in a draft-free place to rise. Allow to rise for 1$^1/_2$ to 2$^1/_2$ hours, until doubled in bulk. Do not rush this step. Yeast should work slowly.

To knead the dough, beat with an electric mixer for 3 minutes. Scatter sesame seeds in bottoms of the loaf pans, especially in corners. Divide the dough between the pans, pushing it into the corners with a spatula and smoothing the tops. Sprinkle with sesame seeds. Allow to rise, uncovered, for 30 to 35 minutes, until the dough just reaches the tops of the pans. Don't let it go higher or it may collapse. Bake at 400°F for 10 minutes. Place foil loosely over the loaves and bake 50 minutes more.

Note: The secret to making yeast-raised gluten-free bread is the xanthan gum.

Makes 2 loaves

Blueberry Oat Muffins

$1^3/_4$ cups barley flour

1 cup quick-cooking oats

$^1/_2$ cup sugar

1 teaspoon baking powder

$^1/_2$ teaspoon baking soda

$^1/_4$ teaspoon sea salt

1 egg

$^1/_2$ cup water

$^1/_3$ cup vegetable oil

1 cup fresh or frozen blueberries

TOPPING

2 tablespoons sugar

$^1/_4$ teaspoon ground nutmeg

Preheat the oven to 400°F. Grease a 12-cup muffin tin or fill with paper liners.

In a bowl, combine the first six ingredients. In another bowl, beat egg, water, and oil. Stir in dry ingredients just until moistened. Fold in blueberries. Fill muffin cups three-fourths full. Combine sugar and nutmeg; sprinkle over muffins. Bake for 18 to 22 minutes or until a toothpick comes out clean. Cool for 5 minutes before removing from pan to a wire rack.

Makes 12 muffins

Corn Muffins

$^3/_4$ cup rice flour

1 cup cornmeal

1 $^1/_2$ tablespoons baking powder

$^1/_2$ teaspoon sea salt

$^1/_4$ cup sugar

1 egg, slightly beaten

$^1/_4$ cup butter or margarine, melted

1 cup water

Preheat the oven to 425°F. Grease a 12-cup muffin tin or fill with paper liners.

In a medium-size bowl, stir together the rice flour, cornmeal, baking powder, salt, and sugar. Add the butter, egg, and water to the dry ingredients and stir until smooth. Fill the muffin cups three-quarters full. Bake for 25 minutes, or until the muffins pull away from the sides of the cups. Remove the muffins from the tin.

Makes 12 muffins

VARIATIONS, IF TOLERATED:
- Substitute an equal amount of milk for the water.

Nut Butter Rice Muffins

1 cup rice flour

2 teaspoons baking powder

1 teaspoon xanthan gum

$^1/_4$ teaspoon sea salt

2 tablespoons maple sugar or sugar

1 tablespoon safflower oil

$^1/_2$ cup nut milk or water

2 tablespoon nut butter

Preheat the oven to 425°F. Grease a 6-cup muffin tin.

Mix the dry ingredients together. Add the oil, nut milk, and nut butter together. Add to the dry ingredients and mix well. Fill the muffin cups three-quarters full. Bake for about 20 minutes.

Makes 6 muffins

VARIATIONS, IF TOLERATED:
- Substitute an equal amount of milk for the nut milk or water.
- Substitute 1$^3/_4$ cups of wheat flour for the rice flour.
- Add 1 egg with the oil and liquid.

Oat Muffins

1 cup sifted oat flour

$3\frac{1}{2}$ teaspoons baking powder

$1\frac{1}{2}$ teaspoons sugar

$\frac{1}{8}$ teaspoon sea salt

$\frac{1}{2}$ teaspoon nutmeg (optional)

$\frac{1}{4}$ cup cold water or oat milk

2 tablespoons oil

Preheat the oven to 425°F. Grease a 6- or 8-cup muffin tin.

Sift the dry ingredients into a medium-size bowl. Add the liquids together. Stir into dry ingredients and mix until smooth. Fill the muffin cups three-quarters full. Bake for 25 minutes.

Makes 6 to 8 muffins

VARIATIONS, IF TOLERATED:
- Substitute an equal amount of milk for the water or oat milk.
- Add 1 egg to the liquid and decrease the baking powder to 2 teaspoons.

Raisin Muffins
- Add $\frac{1}{2}$ cup raisins to the dry ingredients.

Nut Muffins
- Add $\frac{1}{2}$ cup chopped nuts to the dry ingredients.

Banana Oat Muffins
- Add $\frac{1}{2}$ cup mashed ripe banana after the other ingredients are mixed. You may reduce the oat flour to $\frac{3}{4}$ cup and add $\frac{1}{4}$ cup quick oats.

Rice Flour Muffins

$1/2$ cup banana or strawberries, pureed

$1/2$ cup nut milk or water

1 cup rice flour

$1/4$ teaspoon sea salt

$1 1/2$ teaspoons baking powder

1 tablespoon oil

Preheat the oven to 350°F. Grease a 6-cup muffin tin.

   Stir the fruit pulp into the nut milk. Add the dry ingredients and oil. Mix until moistened. Fill the muffin cups three-quarters full. Bake for 15 to 20 minutes.

Makes 6 muffins.

VARIATIONS, IF TOLERATED:
- Substitute an equal amount of milk in place of the nut milk or water.
- Add 1 egg to the liquid and decrease the baking powder to 1 teaspoon.

Almond Biscuits

These biscuits are from the book Bob's Red Mill Baking Book.

1 cup rice flour

$^1/_4$ cup tapioca flour

$^1/_3$ cup potato starch

$^1/_4$ teaspoon xanthan gum

4 teaspoons baking powder

1 teaspoon baking soda

1 teaspoon sugar

2 eggs, slightly beaten

$^1/_3$ cup oil

$^1/_3$ cup water or milk

$^1/_2$ teaspoon almond extract (optional)

$^1/_4$ cup almonds, slivered (optional)

Preheat the oven to 400°F. Lightly grease a baking sheet.

In a large bowl, mix together very thoroughly the dry ingredients. In a medium bowl, beat together the liquids. Add the liquid ingredients to the flour mixture, and stir until combined. Add a small amount of water if the batter is too thick. Stir in the nuts, if desired.

Drop about $^1/_4$ cup dough for each biscuit onto the baking sheet and flatten slightly. Bake for about 12 minutes, or until the biscuits are brown on top.

Makes 12 biscuits

Dried Cherry Spelt Scones

These scones are from the book Bob's Red Mill Baking Book.

$2^{1}/_{4}$ cups spelt flour

$1^{3}/_{4}$ tablespoons baking powder

1 teaspoon baking soda

$^{1}/_{2}$ salt

6 tablespoons butter, chilled and diced

$^{1}/_{2}$ cup cherries, dried and unsulphered

1 egg

$^{1}/_{2}$ cup water or milk

1 teaspoon vanilla

3 tablespoon light brown sugar

Milk or melted butter for glazing

Sugar and ground nutmeg for dusting (optional)

Preheat the oven to 400° F. Lightly grease a baking sheet.

In a food processor or large bowl, pulse or whisk together the flour, baking powder, baking soda, and salt. Cut or pulse in the butter until the mixture resembles coarse crumbs. Remove to a large bowl and stir in the dried cherries.

In another bowl beat together the egg, the water or milk, vanilla, and brown sugar. Stir into the flour mixture until a dough forms.

On a lightly floured surface, knead the dough 8 or 9 times. Pat the dough into a $^{1}/_{2}$ -inch thick round, brush with milk or melted butter, and cut into 6 or 8 wedges. Sprinkle with nutmeg and sugar.

Place the scones on the prepared pan and bake for 15 minutes or until a tester comes out clean. Cool on a wire rack and serve warm or at room temperature.

Makes 6 to 8 servings

Rice Flour Biscuits

$5/8$ cup rice flour

3 teaspoons baking powder

$1/8$ teaspoon sea salt

$1/2$ teaspoon maple sugar or sugar

$1/4$ cup butter or margarine

$1/4$ cup goat's milk, or cow's milk if tolerated

Preheat the oven to 350°F.

Mix the dry ingredients together. Cut in the butter, then stir in the goat's milk. Lightly knead the dough on a board lightly floured with rice flour. Roll out to about $1/2$ inch thick and cut with a 2-inch cookie cutter or glass. Place on an ungreased baking sheet 2 inches apart. Bake for 10 minutes.

Makes 6 to 8 biscuits

Scottish Oatcakes

These oatcakes may be served warm or cold, with butter or jam.

$^2/_3$ cup oatmeal

$^1/_8$ teaspoon sea salt

$^1/_4$ teaspoon baking soda

$^1/_2$ teaspoon nutmeg (optional)

2 tablespoons butter or margarine

1 tablespoon water

Preheat the oven to 400°F. Grease a cookie sheet.

In a medium-size bowl, mix together the oats, salt, baking soda, and nutmeg. In a small saucepan, slowly heat the butter and water until the butter has melted. Bring to a boil, then pour into the oatmeal mixture. Stir to form a soft dough. Mix the dough together with your hands, then turn it onto an oat-floured surface and knead lightly. Roll the dough out thinly to form a circle 8 inches in diameter. Cut the round into 8 wedges. Using a spatula, carefully lift the wedges onto a cookie sheet. Bake for 15 to 20 minutes, or until the oatcakes are crisp, lightly brown, and the edges begin to curl up.

Makes 8 wedges

Oatmeal Crackers

These are the crackers my daughter teethed on when she got her first teeth. I just cooked the crackers longer to make them harder.

1 cup water
$^1/_2$ cup cooking oil
1 teaspoon sea salt
4 cups oat flour

Preheat the oven to 350°F. Grease a cookie sheet.

Combine all the ingredients until stiff dough is formed. Chill. Lightly flour a board and roll out the dough to $^1/_8$ inch thick. Transfer the dough to the cookie sheet. Cut into squares and prick with a fork. Bake for about 20 minutes.

Makes approximately 48 crackers

Rye Crisps

This wafer-thin crisp bread can be eaten as a cracker or as a substitute for bread.

2 cups rye flour
$^1/_2$ teaspoon sea salt
$^1/_4$ cup butter or margarine or oil
$^1/_4$ cup water

Preheat the oven to 400°F. Lightly grease two baking sheets.

In a mixing bowl, combine the rye flour and salt. Cut in the butter or stir in the oil. Stir in the water and mix until the ingredients are thoroughly blended and the dough is firm. Divide the dough in half. Knead each piece lightly on a floured surface. Roll out thinly to about 9 inches square. Cut into 3-inch squares and put the squares on the baking sheets. Prick each square well with a fork to keep it from rising and bubbling. Bake the rye crisps for 10 to 15 minutes, or until the edges just begin to color, but do not let them brown. Cool slightly on the baking sheets, then transfer the crackers to wire racks.

Makes 18 rye crisps

VARIATIONS, IF TOLERATED:
• **Add 1 teaspoon dried mixed herbs to the dry ingredients.**

10.

Cereals and Pancakes

Breakfast doesn't have to be the most difficult meal of the day. Since most people are in a hurry at breakfast time, you'll need to plan ahead and prepare part of the meal ahead of time.

In this chapter you'll find recipes for cereals and pancakes. Try the Apple Nutmeg Crunchy Granola; it's great as a snack too. For other breakfast ideas, see chapter 9 on breads, muffins, crackers, and biscuits. Some puddings can make great morning treats, such as Rice Pudding (see page 298). On days when you are running late, try making a "blender breakfast." Look at chapter 8 for some quick beverage ideas.

Finally, don't limit your breakfast to typical morning meals; warm up tasty leftovers or have some steaming hot homemade soup.

AMARANTH GRANOLA ...149

APPLE NUTMEG CRUNCHY GRANOLA ...150

APPLE OATMEAL ...151

APPLE SPICE OATMEAL ...152

CRUNCHY GRANOLA ...153

DUTCH POTATO PANCAKES ...154

PANCAKE OR WAFFLE BATTER ...155

POTATO PANCAKES ...156

RICE WAFFLES ...157

Amaranth Granola

$^{1}/_{4}$ cup apricot or peach puree

$^{1}/_{4}$ to $^{1}/_{2}$ cup maple syrup

1 tablespoon oil

1 tablespoon vanilla

$^{3}/_{4}$ teaspoon salt

$2^{1}/_{4}$ cups puffed amaranth

$^{1}/_{2}$ cup pine nuts or other variety (optional)

$^{1}/_{2}$ cup raw sunflower seeds

$^{1}/_{2}$ cup unsulfured and diced dried apricots and peaches

$^{1}/_{2}$ cup grated unsweetened coconut

Preheat oven to 375°F. Lightly grease a 13 x 9-inch cake pan.

In a large mixing bow, mix puree, syrup, oil, vanilla, and salt. Add amaranth, nuts, seeds, dried fruit, and coconut. Stir enough to coat dry ingredients. Spread in the cake pan and toast for 20 to 25 minutes, stirring frequently. The edges tend to burn faster than the rest of the granola and so should be watched carefully. Cool and store in an airtight container. Eat within two weeks.

Makes 4 cups

> **VARIATIONS, IF TOLERATED:**
> * Try using other cereals like puffed wild rice or puffed rice from the health food store.

Apple Nutmeg Crunchy Granola

4 cups rolled oats

$^1/_2$ cup coconut, grated or flaked

1 cup finely chopped nuts (optional)

$^1/_2$ cup raw sesame seeds

$^3/_4$ teaspoon sea salt

1 teaspoon nutmeg

$^1/_2$ cup honey

$^1/_3$ cup safflower oil

$^1/_2$ teaspoon vanilla

8 ounces unsulfured dried apples, finely chopped

Preheat the oven to 350°F. Grease two large cookie sheets.

Combine the oats, coconut, nuts, sesame seeds, salt, and nutmeg in a large bowl. In a small saucepan, combine the honey, oil, and vanilla and heat gently to liquefy the honey. Add to the oat mixture and mix thoroughly. Spread on the cookie sheets and bake for 20 to 25 minutes, stirring occasionally. Add the apples. Store in a tightly covered container in the refrigerator.

Makes 8 servings

Apple Oatmeal

1 cup rolled oats

2 cups cold water

$1/2$ teaspoon sea salt

2 apples, peeled, cored, and chopped

Dash of nutmeg

Combine the oats, water, and salt in a saucepan. Cook for 10 minutes over low heat. Add the apples and nutmeg. Cook 5 minutes more, or until the apples are done to the desired consistency. Serve with nut milk and honey.

Makes 4 servings

VARIATIONS, IF TOLERATED:
- Use raisins or dates in place of the apples.

Apple Spice Oatmeal

1 $\frac{1}{2}$ cups apple juice

1 $\frac{1}{2}$ cups water

1 to 1 $\frac{1}{3}$ cups oats, depending on desired thickness

1 apple, peeled and diced

$\frac{1}{2}$ teaspoon nutmeg

$\frac{1}{4}$ cup finely chopped walnuts (optional)

Boil apple juice and water. Add oats; boil over medium high heat 1 to 2 minutes. Add apple and nutmeg. Cook over low heat until oats are done. (The time depends upon the type of oats used.) Sprinkle nuts over the top.

Makes 4 servings

Crunchy Granola

$1/4$ cup unsweetened applesauce

$1/4$ to $1/2$ cup honey

1 tablespoon oil

1 tablespoon vanilla

$3/4$ teaspoon sea salt

$2 1/4$ cups rolled oats

$1/2$ cup chopped almonds or cashews

$1/4$ cup coconut, grated

$1/4$ cup raisins (optional)

Preheat the oven to 375°F.

Mix the applesauce, honey, oil, vanilla, and salt in large bowl. Add the oats, nuts, and coconut. Stir just long enough to coat the dry ingredients. Spread in a 13 x 9-inch pan and bake for 20 to 25 minutes, stirring occasionally. Cool and add the raisins, if desired. Store in an airtight container. Eat within two weeks.

> **Note:** You can add any unsulfured dried fruit, such as cranberries, blueberries, cherries, apples or mangoes. In addition, add any favorite seeds, such as sunflower seeds.

Makes 4 cups

Dutch Potato Pancakes

4 or 5 large potatoes

$1/4$ cup oat flour

$1/4$ teaspoon sea salt

$1/4$ cup coconut milk, nut milk, or goat's milk

Peel the potatoes (if desired) and grate. Make a paste of flour, salt, and milk. Stir into the grated potatoes. Drop into a hot greased pan and fry approximately 5 minutes on each side, until browned and cooked throughout. Serve with butter or margarine and maple syrup.

Makes 4 servings

VARIATIONS, IF TOLERATED:
- Try an equal amount of brown rice flour or wheat flour. Do not use potato starch or tapioca starch as a flour substitute. It turns to rubbery goo!
- Substitute an equal amount of milk for the coconut milk, nut milk, or goat's milk.

Pancake or Waffle Batter

1 cup oat flour

2 teaspoons baking powder

2 tablespoons safflower oil

$^3/_4$ cup fruit juice or water

1 tablespoon maple syrup or maple sugar

Mix the flour and baking powder together. In a separate bowl, combine the juice, oil, and maple syrup and stir lightly. Add to the dry ingredients and stir until well mixed.

Makes 9 pancakes or 4 waffles

VARIATIONS, IF TOLERATED:
- Substitute an equal amount of milk for the fruit juice or water.
- Substitute an equal amount of sugar for the maple sugar.
- Substitute $^7/_8$ cup wheat flour for the oat flour.
- Add 1 egg to the liquids and decrease the baking powder to 1 teaspoon.

Potato Pancakes

1 cup mashed potatoes, seasoned

1 cup finely grated uncooked potatoes

2 tablespoons butter or margarine

$^1/_2$ teaspoon sea salt

$^1/_2$ teaspoon baking powder

Combine all the ingredients and shape into pancakes. A little flour of your choice may be added, if necessary, to hold the cakes together. Sprinkle both sides of the cakes with flour. Heat oil over medium heat. Place the pancakes in the oil and allow the raw potatoes to cook. Serve with maple syrup.

Makes 4 servings

Rice Waffles

2 cups rice flour

4 teaspoons baking powder

1 tablespoon maple sugar

2 cups nut milk or goat's milk

3 tablespoons safflower oil

Sift the dry ingredients together. Mix the nut milk and oil together, combine with the dry ingredients, and gradually stir the mixture until smooth. Bake in a hot waffle iron.

Makes 4 to 6 waffles

VARIATIONS, IF TOLERATED:

- Substitute an equal amount of milk for the nut or goat's milk.
- Substitute an equal amount of sugar for the maple sugar.
- Substitute $2^1/_4$ cups wheat flour for the rice flour.
- Add 1 egg to the liquids and decrease the baking powder to 2 teaspoons.

11.

Salads and Salad Dressings

I love fresh, crisp, green salads with my homemade French Dressing. It certainly beats any bottled salad dressings. I also love making exotic and unusual salads. I try to create new salads by adding fruits, like sliced kiwi, or vegetables, nuts, seeds, or chicken. (In place of chicken, substitute turkey, Cornish hen, duck, goose, or tuna.) Sometimes I make a whole meal out of a salad, and serve a variety of homemade breads. When there are such a variety of ingredients available, you don't feel as though you're making "allergy-free" foods. You're just having fun eating.

SALADS

APPLE GELATIN SALAD ... 161

AVOCADO ALMOND ORANGE SALAD ... 162

AVOCADO STUFFED WITH TUNA ... 163

BANANA HONEY SALAD ... 164

CHICKEN GRAPE SALAD ... 165

CHICKEN RICE SALAD WITH CASHEWS ... 166

CHICKEN SALAD WITH FRESH FRUIT GARNISH ... 167

CHICKEN SALAD WITH GINGER MAYONNAISE ... 168

HAWAIIAN CHICKEN SALAD ... 169

MANDARIN ALMOND SALAD ... 170

MOLDED FRUIT GELATIN ... 171

ORANGE RICE SALAD ... 172

OVERNIGHT COLESLAW ... 173

POTATO SALAD ... 174

SALMON SALAD ... 175

SUNFLOWER SALAD ... 176

SUNNY FRUIT SALAD ... 177

TUNA SALAD ... 178

TUNA SALAD LUAU ... 179

WILD RICE CHICKEN SALAD ... 180

WILD RICE SALAD ... 181

SALAD DRESSINGS

BASIC DRESSING WITH HERBS ... 182

CELERY SEED SALAD DRESSING ... 183

FRENCH DRESSING ... 184

HONEY APPLE DRESSING ... 184

MOCK MAYONNAISE ... 185

PINEAPPLE HONEY DRESSING ... 186

Apple Gelatin Salad

4 cups unsweetened apple juice

3 tablespoons sweetener

$^1/_4$ teaspoon sea salt

2 envelopes unflavored gelatin

5 red eating apples (unpeeled) or
    enough to make 3 cups shredded

$^1/_4$ cup lemon juice

1 teaspoon lemon rind, grated

$^1/_2$ cup finely chopped celery

1 cup chopped walnuts (optional)

Salad greens for garnish

In a medium-size saucepan, combine the apple juice, sweetener, salt, and gelatin. Stir until blended. Heat and stir until the gelatin is dissolved. Remove from the heat and allow to cool. Refrigerate for about 2 hours, until the mixture thickens to the consistency of unbeaten egg whites. Wash the apples. Core and slice one apple, sprinkle with 1 tablespoon lemon juice, and reserve for garnish. Core and shred the remaining apples. Stir in the rest of the lemon juice to keep the apples from turning dark. Sprinkle the lemon rind over the apples. Add the celery and nuts to the apples. Stir the apple mixture into the thickened gelatin. Turn the mixture into a 6-cup mold and refrigerate for 4 to 6 hours, until set. Unmold and serve; garnish with salad greens and the reserved apple slices.

Makes 10 to 12 servings

Avocado Almond Orange Salad

Since I've moved to California, I have fresh and exotic salad ingredients available year-round. I love experimenting with all these unusual ingredients. Try to use multi-colored greens for a more attractive plate. Slivered almonds look good against the dark salad greens, but you can use any nut. You can change the nut oil to match the type of nut you use in the salad. Just make sure the nut oil is fresh! If you can't have oranges, try pineapple. Pour the dressing over the avocado slices right away.

4 cups torn salad greens

2 navel oranges, peeled and sectioned

2 large ripe avocados, peeled and sliced

1 cup seedless grapes, cut in half (optional)

$1/2$ cup chopped nuts (optional)

CITRUS DRESSING

2 tablespoons almond oil

$1/3$ cup oil

$1/4$ cup orange juice

2 tablespoons sugar

1 teaspoon grated orange peel

$1/4$ teaspoon grated nutmeg

On a salad plate, arrange greens, orange, and avocado. Sprinkle grapes and nuts. In a jar with a tight-fitting lid, combine dressing ingredients;

shake well. Drizzle over salad. Serve immediately.

Makes 4 servings

Avocado Stuffed With Tuna

2 ripe avocados

1 (6$^1/_2$-ounce) can solid white tuna, water-packed, drained

1 cup walnuts, chopped (optional)

1 cup mayonnaise

1$^1/_2$ tablespoons tomato paste

Sea salt to taste

Halve and pit the avocados. Scoop out the flesh without tearing the shells.
Dice the flesh into $^1/_2$-inch pieces. In a bowl, mix the drained tuna chunks,
$^2/_3$ cup walnuts, mayonnaise, and tomato paste. Add the avocado. Season
with salt and toss lightly. Divide the salad among the avocado shells and
garnish with the remaining walnuts.

Makes 4 servings

Banana Honey Salad

Lettuce leaves

1 banana

2 teaspoons pineapple juice

$1/4$ cup nut butter

$1/4$ cup honey

1 tablespoon shredded coconut

Arrange lettuce leaves on two salad plates. Slice the banana in half, and then slice lengthwise. Place the banana slices on top of the lettuce leaves. Sprinkle with pineapple juice to keep them from turning dark. Mix the nut butter and honey. Spoon over the banana slices and sprinkle with coconut.

Makes 2 servings

Chicken Grape Salad

2 cups chicken, cooked and cut up

1 cup celery, chopped

1 cup seedless green grapes

$^1/_2$ cup slivered almonds, toasted*

$1 ^3/_4$ cups mayonnaise

1 tablespoon lemon juice

$^1/_2$ teaspoon sea salt

In medium bowl, combine all ingredients; mix well. Serve on a bed of lettuce or make into a sandwich.

Makes 6 to 8 servings

> *Tip: To toast almonds, spread on cookie sheet. Bake at 350°F about 10 minutes, stirring occasionally.

Chicken Rice Salad with Cashews

3 cups chicken, diced and cooked

$^1/_2$ cup celery, diced

3 cups cooked rice

1 cup mayonnaise

1 tablespoon lemon juice

1 teaspoon sweetener

1 teaspoon sea salt

$^1/_2$ cup cashews, raw or roasted

Salad greens for garnish

Combine the chicken, celery, and rice in a large bowl. In a small bowl, combine the mayonnaise, lemon juice, sweetener, and salt; mix well. Pour the dressing over the chicken mixture and toss lightly but thoroughly. Adjust the seasonings; mix lightly. Refrigerate, covered, for about 2 hours before serving to blend the flavors. Just before serving, add the cashews and mix lightly. Serve on crisp salad greens.

Makes 6 servings

Chicken Salad with Fresh Fruit Garnish

Serve with fresh fruit, such as strawberries, melon slices, pineapple chunks, and orange slices.

4 cups cooked and diced chicken

1 cup finely chopped celery

1 tablespoon lemon juice

1 cup slivered almonds, toasted

$1\,^1/_2$ teaspoons sea salt

$1\,^1/_2$ cups seedless green grapes

$^3/_4$ cup heavy cream, whipped

$1\,^1/_2$ cups mayonnaise

Lettuce, washed, dried, and chilled

Combine chicken, celery, lemon juice, almonds, salt, and grapes. Toss and refrigerate for at least 1 hour or until well chilled. Just before serving, whip cream, fold into mayonnaise, then fold into chicken mixture. Serve chicken on a bed of lettuce garnished with fresh fruit.

Makes 6 to 8 servings

Chicken Salad with Ginger Mayonnaise

GINGER MAYONNAISE

$\frac{1}{2}$ cup mayonnaise

$\frac{1}{2}$ cup sour cream

1 tablespoon apple vinegar

1 teaspoon ground ginger

$\frac{1}{2}$ teaspoon dry mustard

3 to 4 tablespoons minced crystallized or candied ginger

CHICKEN SALAD

4 cups cooked and cubed chicken

2 cups chopped celery

1 cup julienned jicama or water chestnuts

1 apple (1 cup), peeled, cored, and cubed

$\frac{3}{4}$ cup slivered almonds, toasted for garnish

In small bowl, prepare the Ginger Mayonnaise. Whisk together mayonnaise and sour cream until blended. Whisk in apple vinegar, ground ginger, and dry mustard until smooth. Stir in crystallized ginger. Set aside.

In large bowl, prepare the chicken salad. Combine chicken, celery, water chestnuts, and apple. Spoon Ginger Mayonnaise over Chicken Salad. Toss gently to mix. Cover and refrigerate at least 2 hours or until serving time. Garnish with almonds.

Makes 6 servings

Hawaiian Chicken Salad

1 (15-ounce) can mandarin oranges

1 cup pineapple chunks

1 cup chopped celery

3 cups cooked and diced chicken

$1/2$ cup slivered almonds, toasted

DRESSING

1 cup mayonnaise

$1/2$ teaspoon sea salt

$1/4$ teaspoon sage

2 tablespoons orange juice

In a large bowl, gently mix the fruit, celery, chicken, and almonds. In a smaller bowl, mix together all the dressing ingredients and pour over chicken salad. Carefully mix together and chill before serving.

Makes 6 servings

Mandarin Almond Salad

3 tablespoons brown sugar

$^1/_2$ cup almonds, slivered

1 head romaine lettuce, torn into bite-size pieces

$^1/_2$ head iceberg lettuce, torn into bite-size pieces

$^3/_4$ cup celery, chopped

2 tablespoons apple vinegar

$^1/_4$ cup oil

2 tablespoons chopped fresh parsley

$^1/_2$ teaspoon sea salt

1 tablespoon sugar (optional)

1 (11-ounce) can mandarin oranges, drained

In a saucepan over medium heat, melt sugar until pale caramel in color. Add almonds and stir to coat. Remove from heat and pour on foil to cool. Chop when cooled. Set aside. In a large salad bowl combine lettuce and celery. In a small bowl mix together vinegar, oil, parsley, salt, and sugar; refrigerate. When ready to serve, add the almonds, mandarin oranges, and dressing to the lettuce mixture and toss.

Makes 4 to 6 servings

Molded Fruit Gelatin

1 envelope unflavored gelatin

$^{1}/_{4}$ cup cold water

1 cup hot water

$^{1}/_{2}$ cup unsweetened pineapple, grape, or apple juice

Sweetener to taste

Pinch of sea salt

1 cup fruit (optional)

Soften the gelatin in the cold water. Add the hot water and stir until dissolved. Add the juice, sweetener, and salt. Pour into a mold and add the fruit after the gelatin has thickened slightly. Chill until firm. Serve in lettuce cups, if desired.

Makes 4 servings

VARIATIONS, IF TOLERATED:
- Add 2 cups diced tart apples, $^{1}/_{2}$ cup chopped pecans, and $^{1}/_{2}$ cup diced celery to the gelatin mixture and pour into the mold.

Orange Rice Salad

3 tablespoons wine vinegar

5 tablespoons allowed oil, such as safflower oil

3 tablespoons orange juice

1 tablespoon chopped fresh parsley

4 cups warm cooked rice

2 oranges or 2 cans mandarin oranges, well drained

1 celery stalk, thinly sliced

$^{1}/_{2}$ cup seedless raisins

$^{1}/_{2}$ cup chopped walnuts (optional)

Pour the wine vinegar into a small bowl and add the oil, 1 tablespoon at a time, beating vigorously with a fork after each addition. Add the orange juice and parsley and beat again. Put the warm cooked rice into a large mixing bowl. Add $^{1}/_{3}$ cup of the dressing and mix thoroughly. The warm rice will absorb the dressing. Peel and remove the pith from the oranges. Cut away the membrane from the segments of fruit. Add the orange segments or mandarin oranges to the rice along with the celery, raisins, and nuts. Mix well. Chill before serving. This salad will keep well in the refrigerator for up to two days. Add more dressing before serving.

Makes 4 to 6 servings

Overnight Coleslaw (MAYONNAISE-FREE)

8 cups cabbage, shredded

2 carrots, shredded

¾ cup sugar

DRESSING

2 teaspoons sugar

1 teaspoon dry mustard

1 teaspoon celery seed

1 teaspoon sea salt

1 cup vinegar

¾ cup vegetable oil

In a large bowl, combine cabbage and carrots. Sprinkle with sugar; set aside.

In a saucepan, combine dressing ingredients; bring to a boil. Remove from the heat and pour over vegetables, stirring to cover evenly. Cover and refrigerate overnight. Stir well before serving.

Makes 8 servings

Potato Salad

6 cups potatoes (6 medium), cooked, peeled, and cubed

$^3/_4$ cup chopped celery (1 large stalk)

$1 ^1/_2$ cups hard-boiled eggs, sliced (optional)

$^1/_3$ cup mayonnaise

1 teaspoon sea salt

$^1/_4$ cup sunflower seeds

In a large bowl, combine all the ingredients except the sunflower seeds. Toss gently until well mixed. Refrigerate. Just before serving, toss with the sunflower seeds.

Makes 6 servings

Salmon Salad

2 cups canned salmon (packed in water), drained

$1/4$ cup thinly sliced carrots

1 cup diced celery

1 cup mayonnaise

$1/2$ teaspoon sea salt

Mix all the ingredients together. Serve over lettuce or on sandwiches.

Makes 3 cups

Sunflower Salad

2 cups coarsely shredded carrots

1 cup thinly sliced celery

2 firm bananas, sliced

$^1/_2$ cup sunflower seeds

$^1/_4$ cup sunflower or safflower oil

2 tablespoons unsweetened pineapple juice

$^1/_4$ teaspoon sea salt

Crisp lettuce cups

Combine the carrots, celery, bananas, and sunflower seeds. In a separate bowl, stir together the oil, pineapple juice, and salt. Pour over the salad mixture and toss lightly. Serve in lettuce cups.

Makes 4 servings

Sunny Fruit Salad

2 tablespoons orange juice

2 tablespoons lemon juice

$^1/_2$ teaspoon sea salt

2 teaspoons sweetener

1 cup grated carrots

1 cup grated cabbage

1 cup chopped unpeeled apples

Combine the orange juice, lemon juice, salt, and sweetener. Mix the carrots, cabbage, and apples together. Pour the juices over the salad and toss.

Makes 6 servings

Tuna Salad

2 (6-ounce) cans white chunk tuna (packed in water), drained

1 tablespoon fresh lemon juice

1 (8-ounce) can crushed pineapple, well-drained

Dash celery salt

$^2/_3$ cup mayonnaise

$^1/_2$ cup shredded carrots

$^1/_2$ cup green grapes or raisins

$^1/_3$ cup slivered almonds

Lettuce leaves

In medium bowl, combine tuna, lemon juice, pineapple, and celery salt; toss. Fold in mayonnaise, carrots, grapes, and almonds. Serve in lettuce-lined bowl.

Tip: Can also be served on crackers as a party snack.

Makes 3 to 4 servings

Tuna Salad Luau

3/4 cup mayonnaise

3/4 teaspoon curry powder

2 (6-ounce) cans flaked tuna (packed in water), drained

1 (20-ounce) can pineapple chunks, drained

1 cup sliced celery

1/2 cup chopped walnuts (optional)

1 tablespoon chopped fresh parsley

Sea salt to taste

Lettuce leaves

Mix the mayonnaise with the curry powder. Combine the remaining ingredients except the salt and lettuce leaves in a separate bowl. Add the mayonnaise mixture and season to taste. Toss lightly. Chill until ready to serve. Serve on lettuce.

Makes 4 to 6 servings

Wild Rice Chicken Salad

2 1/2 cups cooked wild rice (3/4 cup uncooked)

1 cup chopped celery

1 (8-ounce) can pineapple chunks, drained

1 cup halved green grapes

1/2 cup mandarin oranges, drained

1 cup chopped cashews or walnuts (optional)

2 1/2 cups cooked and diced chicken

3/4 cup light mayonnaise

1 teaspoon sage

1/2 teaspoon sea salt

In large bowl, toss wild rice with celery, pineapple, grapes, oranges, nuts, and chicken. In small bowl, combine mayonnaise, sage, and salt. Toss mayonnaise with salad mixture. Cover and refrigerate several hours or overnight.

Makes 8 to 10 servings

Wild Rice Salad

1 cup uncooked wild rice

Sea salt (optional)

2 cups cooked and diced chicken

1 $^1/_2$ cups halved green grapes

1 cup sliced water chestnuts, drained

$^3/_4$ cup mayonnaise

1 cup cashews (optional)

Lettuce leaves

Cook rice according to package directions, adding salt if desired. Drain well; cool to room temperature. Spoon into a large bowl; add chicken, grapes, water chestnuts, and mayonnaise. Toss gently with a fork. Cover and chill. Just before serving, add cashews if desired. Serve on lettuce leaves.

Makes 6 servings

Basic Dressing With Herbs

Plan to make several variations of this basic dressing whenever you prepare it. Pour a measured portion of the basic ingredients into the blender; add another special ingredient of your choice. Blend and pour the contents into a refrigerator-storage jar. Then pour another measured portion of the basic ingredients into the blender and add a different special ingredient of your choice. Blend and pour contents into another refrigerator-storage jar. Repeat this preparation several times. You will have made several different dressings quickly and easily, and you will have a choice of dressings for your daily salads. Don't forget to label each salad dressing.

2 cups vegetable oil (your favorite)

1 cup vinegar (your favorite)

1 teaspoon herbs and seasonings (your favorites)

Combine all the ingredients in a bowl and whisk until smooth.

Makes 3 cups of dressing

Celery Seed Salad Dressing (MAYONNAISE-FREE)

$^1/_2$ cup sugar

1 teaspoon dry mustard

2 teaspoons sea salt

$^1/_2$ cup vinegar

1 cup salad oil

2 teaspoons celery seed

Combine sugar, mustard, salt, and vinegar and stir well. Add the oil very slowly and beat well. Stir in celery seed. Let dressing stand 24 hours before using.

Makes 1 $^1/_2$ pints

French Dressing (MAYONNAISE-FREE)

This is my favorite salad dressing; I always have it on hand!

$^1/_2$ cup safflower oil

$^1/_3$ cup apple cider vinegar

$^1/_3$ cup homemade catsup (see page 304)

   OR 2 tablespoons tomato paste

$^1/_4$ cup honey

$^1/_2$ teaspoon sea salt

Mix together and shake well before pouring on salad.

Makes 1 $^1/_2$ cups

Honey Apple Dressing

2 tablespoons honey

$^1/_4$ cup apple juice

$^1/_2$ cup safflower oil

Mix the ingredients together well. Season to taste with salt and herbs as desired.

Makes 1 cup

Mock Mayonnaise

This recipe is actually a variation on the basic dressing, but it is thicker and creamier. It is risky to use real homemade mayonnaise—which requires uncooked eggs—due to the prevalence of salmonellosis. The pathogen salmonella is frequently found in raw egg and can cause serious gastrointestinal upsets. This mock mayonnaise, made without raw egg, is a good substitute for regular mayonnaise. Try different flavors of oil if you like and/or use different seasonings. Keep refrigerated since it has sour cream. Use a product like Daisy Brand Sour Cream, which is 100% natural cultured cream without any fillers.

1 cup oil

$^1/_2$ cup vinegar

1 cup sour cream

1 teaspoon herbs and seasoning

Combine oil, vinegar, and sour cream in a bowl and blend until smooth. Add herbs and seasonings of your choice to vary the dressing.

Makes 3 cups of thick dressing

Pineapple Honey Dressing

$^1/_2$ cup honey

$^1/_4$ cup pineapple juice

$^1/_4$ teaspoon sea salt

3 tablespoons crushed pineapple

Combine all the ingredients. Mix well and serve over fruit salad or greens.

Makes 1 cup

12.

Soups and Stews

Thank goodness for the invention of electric slow cookers. After dinner, I add to a cooker ingredients such as chicken or beef, carrots, celery, celery leaves, and seasonings and let it simmer for a few hours. I refrigerate it overnight. The next morning I remove the fat from the stock, and add some potatoes, rice, and/or beans, and a dash of salt. I let the soup cook slowly until evening. When I come home at night, I am met by the wonderful aroma of homemade soup ready to be served.

Since homemade soups don't have all the preservatives canned soups have, remember to use the soups and stews quickly if refrigerated. Otherwise, you can freeze them. Try freezing the broths, soups, and stews in muffin tins, reheating them in a microwave-safe cup. It's just the right amount.

As you can see, homemade soups don't have to take up much of your time, and the taste surpasses that of canned soup.

BEEF AND VEGETABLE STEW ... 189

BEEF STOCK ... 190

CHICKEN AND POTATO SOUP ... 191

CHICKEN SOUP ... 192

CHICKEN BROTH ... 193

CORN CHOWDER ... 194

CREAM OF VEGETABLE SOUP ... 195

CREAMY POTATO SOUP ... 196

GREEK LEMON SOUP ... 197

MINESTRONE ... 198

NAVY BEAN SOUP ... 199

PEA SOUP ... 200

TOMATO SOUP ... 201

VEGETABLE BEEF SOUP ... 202

Beef and Vegetable Stew

This is a quick five-minute dish. You can open a can of sliced, drained potatoes and carrots or use frozen ones. I like to add a touch of sugar to canned tomato products to cut down the acidity of the tomato flavor just a bit. Use lean beef so your dish won't become too greasy.

2 medium potatoes, sliced

2 medium carrots, sliced

1 (29-ounce) can whole tomatoes, drained and broken up (reserve liquid)

$\frac{1}{3}$ cup uncooked rice

1 pound lean ground beef or lean beef stew meat

1 teaspoon sugar, stirred into tomatoes (optional)

$\frac{1}{2}$ sea salt, or to taste

Preheat the oven to 350°F.

Layer the vegetables and beef in the order given in a greased 2-quart casserole. Season each layer with salt. Sprinkle the reserved tomato liquid over the finished layers. Bake, covered, for 45 minutes to an hour.

Makes 4 servings

VARIATIONS, IF TOLERATED:

- *Just before adding the ground beef, add 1 cup cooked kidney beans (drained). Or substitute browned pure pork sausage for the ground beef.*

Beef Stock

Use this stock in all recipes requiring beef stock. You can use the meat from these bones for something else, such as the Minestrone soup on page 198.

6 pounds beef soup bones
2 $\frac{1}{2}$ quarts water
2 teaspoons sea salt
1 cup sliced carrots
$\frac{1}{2}$ cup chopped celery with leaves
1 large bay leaf
1 tablespoon parsley

Put the soup bones, water, salt, carrots, celery, bay leaf, and parsley in a kettle. Simmer, uncovered, for 2 to 3 hours, taking care not to boil, until the broth has a pleasant taste. Remove the bay leaf. Remove the meat from the bones and cut up. Set this meat aside for another beef soup recipe. Strain. Skim off excess fat or chill the stock overnight and then lift off the fat layer. Freeze in 1 or 2 cup portions and thaw as needed.

Makes 6 cups

Chicken and Potato Soup

2 cups chicken broth (see page 193)

1 cup cooked and diced chicken

1 cup cooked and diced potatoes

Sea salt to taste

$^1/_2$ teaspoon sage

Parsley flakes (optional)

In a heavy saucepan, combine the stock, chicken, potatoes, salt, and sage. Bring to a boil, stirring constantly. Add additional water or chicken broth, for the desired consistency. Add salt if needed. Serve with parsley sprinkled on top.

Makes 6 servings

Chicken Soup

1 (3-pound) chicken, cut up

6 cups water

2 teaspoons sea salt

1 bay leaf

1 teaspoon sage

1 teaspoon thyme

1 tablespoon dried parsley

6 carrots, chopped

3 stalks celery, chopped

1 cup uncooked rice or barley

Place the chicken in a large stock pot. Cover with water and add all the seasonings plus 1 carrot and 1 stalk celery. Cover, bring to a boil, and simmer for 1 hour, or until the chicken is tender. When the chicken is done, remove it from the stock pot. Strain the broth and discard the vegetables. Refrigerate overnight and skim the fat from the top of the broth. Skin and bone the chicken and cut the meat into small pieces. Reheat the broth, add the remaining vegetables, and cook for 15 to 20 minutes, or until the vegetables are almost tender. Add the diced, cooked chicken and rice or barley to the broth and cook for an additional 15 minutes.

Makes 8 servings

Chicken Broth

4 pounds chicken bones or whole carcass, broken up

4 quarts cold water

1 teaspoon sage

1 teaspoon thyme

1 tablespoon dried parsley

1 carrot, diced

Several stalks celery, diced

Sea salt to taste

Cover the chicken bones or carcass with cold water in a heavy-bottomed saucepan. Add the sage, thyme, parsley, carrot, celery, and salt and bring slowly to a boil. Simmer for 2 to 3 hours. Strain, season, and cool. Refrigerate. Skim off the layer of fat on top when chilled. Freeze in 1 to 2 cup portions. Don't keep in refrigerator unless you will be using it within two to three days at the most. The chicken broth can spoil easily.

Makes 2 quarts

Corn Chowder

2 cups boiling water

2 cups canned corn

2 cups diced potatoes

1 teaspoon sea salt

2 cups milk or milk substitute

Into boiling water, add vegetables and salt. Cook until tender. Remove from the heat and slowly stir in the milk. Reheat, but do not boil, and serve at once.

Makes 4 to 6 servings

Cream of Vegetable Soup

This tastes so much better if you can use real butter as the base for this dish.

$^1/_4$ *cup butter*

3 tablespoons flour or rice flour

2 cups milk

2 cups chicken broth (see page 193)

Dash of sea salt

1 teaspoon sage

2 teaspoons parsley

1 teaspoon thyme

2 cups cooked vegetables and/or meat chunks

In a heavy saucepan, stir the butter and flour together over low heat. Gradually add the milk, stirring constantly. When the mixture begins to boil, add the chicken broth and continue to stir until well mixed and hot. Puree the vegetables in a blender. Add the salt, seasonings, pureed vegetables and the meat chunks, if using. Cook until hot.

Makes 6 to 8 servings

Creamy Potato Soup

Most people think a creamy potato soup must be made with the wonderful white sauce known as the roux. However, this soup is thickened by using leftover mashed potatoes. The salt is written "to taste," since there may be salt already in the mashed potatoes.

2 cups cooked mashed potatoes

4 cups milk or substitute, divided

2 tablespoons butter (optional)

Sea salt to taste

1 cup shredded cheese (optional)

Parsley flakes (optional)

Combine mashed potatoes and $1^1/_2$ cups milk. If desired, blend potatoes and milk in blender for smoother consistency. Pour into a 6-quart pan. Add remaining $2^1/_2$ cups milk, butter, and salt. Simmer until heated or it is at the right consistency for you. Sprinkle cheese and parsley on top, if desired.

> **VARIATIONS:**
> * Use potato soup as cream soup base and add 2 cups cooked cubed potatoes, $^1/_2$ cup each cooked celery, carrots, and any other cooked vegetable you like.

Makes 6 to 8 servings

Greek Lemon Soup

Here's the secret to making this soup: dilute the egg yolk mixture with a cup of the hot broth first, and then don't boil the soup again. It took me a long time to get real Greek lemon soup and not soup with scrambled eggs.

6 cups chicken broth (see page 193)

$^1\!/_2$ cup uncooked rice

Sea salt to taste

3 egg yolks

$^1\!/_4$ cup lemon juice

2 tablespoons chopped fresh parsley

In a large pan, bring the chicken broth to a boil. Add the rice, season with salt, and cook until the rice is tender, 15 to 20 minutes. In a medium-size bowl, beat the egg yolks until light and frothy. Slowly add the lemon juice, beating well. Just before serving, dilute the egg-lemon mixture with 1 cup hot broth, beating constantly with a whisk until well blended. Gradually add the diluted mixture to the remaining hot soup, stirring constantly. Bring almost to the boiling point; do not boil or the soup will curdle. Stir in the parsley and season to taste.

Makes 6 servings

Minestrone

2 tablespoons oil

2 cups sliced celery

2 cups sliced carrots

2 teaspoons dried oregano

2 teaspoons dried basil

6 cups beef stock (see page 190) or water

3 cups cooked beans, such as pintos,
    kidney beans, or limas (one kind or mixed)

1 (8-ounce) can mushrooms, sliced

2 cups homemade tomato sauce (see page 307)
    OR 4 cups canned tomatoes

$1/2$ cup chopped fresh parsley

1 tablespoon apple cider vinegar

1 teaspoon honey (optional)

3 cups cooked beef (optional)

2 cups cooked rice

In a large 6-quart pan over medium heat, combine the oil, celery, and carrots. Cook, stirring occasionally, for 10 minutes. Add the oregano and basil. Add the stock or water, beans, mushrooms, and tomato sauce or tomatoes. Simmer gently for 30 minutes. Add the parsley, vinegar, and honey. Simmer for 5 minutes. Add the beef and cooked rice, heat, and serve.

Makes 12 servings

Navy Bean Soup

2 cups chicken or beef stock (see page 190)

2 cups water

$^1/_2$ cup dried navy beans

1 bay leaf

1 cup diced carrots

1 cup diced celery

In a large stock pot, combine the stock and water. Bring to a boil and add the beans and bay leaf. Lower the heat and simmer the ingredients for approximately 2 hours. Remove the bay leaf and add the carrots and celery. Simmer for another 30 minutes. Put the mixture in a blender to puree, if desired. Return the soup to the pot and add enough water to thin it to the desired consistency. Reheat to boiling and serve.

Makes 6 to 8 servings

Pea Soup

2 cups fresh peas (or 1 10-ounce package frozen)

2 tablespoons finely chopped carrots

2 tablespoons finely diced celery

$^1/_8$ teaspoon dried sweet basil

1 cup chicken broth

Boil the fresh peas, carrots, and celery until tender or prepare frozen peas according to the package directions. Puree the peas, carrots, and celery in a blender with the water in which they were cooked. Add the basil and blend well. Combine the chicken broth with the puree and reheat to the boiling point.

Makes 4 servings

Tomato Soup

1 (6-ounce) can tomato paste

2 cups chicken or beef stock (see page 190)

$^1/_2$ teaspoon sea salt

$^1/_4$ cup finely chopped celery

1 tablespoon honey

In a large saucepan, mix all the ingredients. Bring to a boil and simmer for 5 minutes.

Makes 4 servings

VARIATIONS, IF TOLERATED:
- Substitute an equal amount of sugar for the honey.
- Substitute an equal amount of milk for the chicken stock.

Vegetable Beef Soup

4 pounds beef soup bones

8 cups water

1 bay leaf

1 teaspoon sea salt

1 cup diced potatoes

1 cup diced carrots

1 cup diced cabbage or chopped tomatoes

1 cup diced celery

2 cups cooked rice, barley, or allowed noodles

Cook the soup bones in the water with the bay leaf and salt for approximately 2 hours. Add the vegetables, cover, and simmer for 1 hour more. Remove the bones and bay leaf. Remove any meat from the bone and add to the soup. Refrigerate overnight, skim off the fat, reheat, and add the rice, barley, or noodles. Cook until heated thoroughly.

Makes 12 servings

13.

Vegetables and Side Dishes

Even for the person with food allergies, there is still a large selection of vegetable dishes available. Try Baked Sweet Potato Casserole, Confetti Rice, Oriental Tomato Skillet, Braised Celery, or Dilled Carrots. Besides adding valuable nutrients to your diet, they add color and variety.

BAKED SWEET POTATO CASSEROLE ...205

BARLEY AND MUSHROOM PILAF ...206

BRAISED CELERY ...207

CHINA BOWL RICE STICKS ...208

CONFETTI RICE ...209

STUFFED MUSHROOMS ...210

CUCUMBER NOODLES ...211

DATE YAM SUPREME ...212

DILLED CARROTS ...213

EGGPLANT WITH TOMATO ...214

GREEN BEANS WITH ALMONDS ...215

HASH BROWN POTATOES ...216

MAPLE APPLE SWEET POTATO BAKE ...217

MAPLE CARROTS ...218

OATMEAL STUFFING ...219

ORANGE VEGETABLE KABOBS ...220

ORIENTAL TOMATO SKILLET ...221

RICE PILAF ...222

CRANBERRY RELISH ...223

Baked Sweet Potato Casserole

$1/2$ cup maple syrup

$1/2$ cup unsweetened crushed pineapple, well-drained

$1/2$ cup raisins

$1/4$ teaspoon sea salt

2 cups cooked sweet potatoes, cubed

2 tablespoons butter or margarine

$1/4$ to $1/2$ cup almonds, slivered

Preheat the oven to 350°F.

Combine the syrup, pineapple, raisins, and salt. Arrange the potatoes in a 1-quart dish. Spread the fruit mixture on top. Dot with butter and sprinkle with almonds. Bake for 40 to 45 minutes.

Makes 6 to 8 servings

Barley and Mushroom Pilaf

It is best to prepare this dish the day before serving so that the barley can soak overnight in the stock.

2 tablespoons oil

1 cup sliced fresh mushrooms

$^1/_4$ cup pearl barley

2 cups well-seasoned chicken broth (see page 193)

Sea salt to taste

1 bay leaf

Heat the oil in a frying pan over medium heat. Add mushrooms and sauté for 1 minute, stirring constantly. Add pearl barley and fry for 1 minute more, stirring occasionally. Transfer barley mixture to an ovenproof dish. Pour in broth. Season with salt. Put the bay leaf on top, cover the dish, and refrigerate for at least 2 hours, preferably overnight.

Preheat the oven to 375°F. Bake the casserole, covered, for 1 hour, or until the stock is absorbed and the barley is tender and slightly chewy. Remove the bay leaf. Serve immediately.

Makes 4 servings

VARIATIONS, IF TOLERATED:
- **Sprinkle with $^1/_4$ cup grated cheddar cheese just before serving.**

Braised Celery

1 bunch celery

$1/4$ cup allowed oil

1 cup homemade chicken or beef stock (see page 190)

Sea salt to taste

Chopped parsley for garnish

Wash and separate the stalks of celery, removing the leaves. Cut them crosswise, on a slant, into 2-inch lengths. In a large skillet, heat the oil and sauté the celery over high heat for about 2 minutes, stirring constantly. Turn to medium, add the stock, cover tightly, and steam for 10 minutes, or until the celery is tender but still firm. Add salt and garnish with parsley.

Makes 4 to 6 servings

China Bowl Rice Sticks

Rice sticks (also known as cellophane noodles) are prepared in three basic ways.

Boiled: Add 7 ounces of rice sticks to 3 quarts of rapidly boiling water. Cook for 3 minutes and drain.

Stir-fried: Soak rice sticks in hot water for 10 minutes. Drain. Cut into 2-inch lengths. Add to stir fries or soups.

Deep-fried: Drop small amounts of dry rice sticks into safflower oil heated to 375°F. The sticks will instantly puff up. Skim them off, drain, and use as a crunchy garnish. Particularly good in a chicken or tuna salad.

Confetti Rice

$^1/_4$ cup butter or margarine

$1^1/_2$ cups rice, uncooked

3 cups chicken broth, hot (see page 193)

$^3/_4$ cup chopped fresh parsley

$^3/_4$ cup shredded carrot

$^3/_4$ cup chopped celery (1 large stalk)

$^3/_4$ cup sliced mushrooms

$^3/_4$ cup slivered and toasted almonds (optional)

Sea salt to taste

Preheat the oven to 350°F.

In a heavy skillet, melt the butter over medium heat. Add the rice and toss to coat. Heat the rice in the butter for 5 minutes, stirring occasionally. Combine the rice and chicken broth in a 2-quart casserole. Cover and bake for 45 minutes. Stir in the parsley, carrot, celery, mushrooms, and almonds. Continue to bake for 10 minutes more.

Makes 6 to 8 servings

Stuffed Mushrooms

32 large fresh mushrooms

$1/4$ cup butter or margarine

4 slices Oatmeal Bread, cubed (see page 130)

1 (4-ounce) can water chestnuts, finely chopped

$1/2$ teaspoon sage

$1/2$ teaspoon oregano powder

$1/2$ teaspoon thyme powder

Sea salt to taste

$2 1/2$ tablespoons chopped fresh parsley

2 tablespoons chopped walnuts (optional)

Wash and dry the mushrooms. Remove and chop the stems. Lay the caps upside down in a well-greased 8-inch-square baking dish. In a small skillet, melt the butter. Add the mushroom stems, cubed bread, and water chest-nuts and sauté lightly. Transfer to a small bowl, add the sage, oregano, thyme, salt, parsley, and walnuts, and mix thoroughly. Fill each cap with a rounded teaspoon of the mixture. Heat under a broiler for 3 to 5 minutes, until bubbly. Serve immediately.

> Note: You can add other ingredients like dried cranberries, diced celery or shredded cheese—anything that you would add to a stuffing mix.

Makes 6 to 8 servings

Cucumber Noodles

This recipe was inspired by one I came across in Gourmet *magazine. Although I couldn't sample the recipe, due to my allergies, my volunteer cooks adapted this recipe and rated it an A+. For the freshly chopped herbs, try oregano, basil, mint, parsley, rosemary, or thyme, depending on what you are serving with it.*

3 seedless cucumbers ($2^{1}/_{2}$ to $2^{3}/_{4}$ pounds total), peeled

2 tablespoons unsalted butter

2 tablespoons finely chopped fresh herbs (optional)

$^{1}/_{2}$ teaspoon sea salt

$^{1}/_{2}$ teaspoon finely grated lemon zest

1 teaspoon fresh lemon juice

Using an adjustable peeler, slice each cucumber lengthwise into long $^{1}/_{8}$-inch-thick julienne strips, slicing until you reach the core, then rotate cucumber a quarter turn and continue slicing and rotating until left with nothing but core. Blanch cucumber "noodles" in a 4-quart pot of boiling salted water for 1 minute, then drain in a colander. Immerse colander with cucumbers in a large bowl of cold water to stop cooking, about 2 minutes. Drain cucumbers, then transfer to a clean kitchen towel and pat cucumbers dry. Heat butter in a 10-inch heavy skillet over moderate heat until foam subsides, then mix cucumbers, herbs, salt, zest, and lemon juice, tossing to coat, until just heated through, about 1 minute.

Makes 4 servings

Date Yam Supreme

2 cups yams or sweet potatoes, cooked until tender

$^1/_4$ to $^1/_2$ cup milk or substitute

3 tablespoons butter or margarine

1 cup pecans

1 cup bananas, mashed

1 cup dates, chopped

$^1/_2$ cup honey

1 tablespoon orange juice

$^1/_4$ teaspoon sea salt

Preheat oven to 350°F.

Combine yams with milk or substitute and butter or margarine. Beat until fluffy. Stir in remaining ingredients. Pour into a greased casserole dish. Bake 20 to 25 minutes. Put under broiler a few minutes to brown top, if desired.

Makes 4 servings

Dilled Carrots

$^3/_4$ pound carrots, sliced thin

$^1/_2$ cup apple juice

1 $^1/_2$ teaspoons butter, oil, or margarine

1 teaspoon maple syrup

2 teaspoons arrowroot or cornstarch

$^1/_4$ cup apple juice

1 teaspoon dill weed, dried

In a heavy saucepan with lid, simmer the carrots in the apple juice until tender, about 12 to 15 minutes. If the juice boils away, add a little water to prevent sticking. Add the butter and maple syrup. In a small bowl, mix the arrowroot and $^1/_4$ cup apple juice. Stir into the pan and cook, stirring, for 2 minutes, until the sauce is thick and clear. Stir in the dill weed.

Makes 4 to 6 servings

Eggplant with Tomato

1 $^1/_2$ cups cubed eggplant

1 cup canned tomatoes

Sea salt to taste

$^1/_4$ to $^1/_2$ cup crushed puffed-rice cereal

1 tablespoon butter, margarine, or oil

Preheat the oven to 400°F.

Soak the eggplant in water for about 30 minutes; cook in boiling water until tender, then drain. Add the tomatoes. Place in a casserole; add salt. Brown the crushed cereal in the tablespoon of butter over medium heat. Sprinkle over the top of the casserole. Bake for about 15 minutes.

Makes 6 to 8 servings

VARIATIONS, IF TOLERATED:

- In place of crushed puffed rice cereal, use crushed corn flakes or cracker crumbs.

Green Beans with Almonds

2 pounds green beans

$^1/_2$ teaspoon sea salt

$^1/_2$ cup boiling water

$^1/_4$ cup blanched and slivered almonds

2 tablespoons allowed oil

$^1/_4$ cup chopped fresh parsley

Wash and dry the beans and cut into 1-inch pieces. Add the salt and beans to the boiling water. Quickly return to a boil. Reduce the heat to low and steam until tender (7 to 10 minutes). Drain the vegetables. Stir in the almonds, oil, and parsley.

Makes 6 servings

Hash Brown Potatoes

5 to 6 medium potatoes

1 teaspoon sea salt

$^1/_3$ cup oil

Cook the unpeeled potatoes in water. Chill for 2 hours, then peel and shred to make 4 cups. In a large bowl, combine the potatoes and salt. Heat the oil in a skillet. Pat the potatoes into the pan, leaving a $^1/_2$-inch space around the edge. Cover and brown for 10 to 12 minutes. Check the potatoes, reduce the heat if necessary, and cook 8 to 10 minutes longer, until golden. Place a platter over the pan and invert to place the potatoes on it.

Makes 8 servings

Maple Apple Sweet Potato Bake

$^1/_2$ cup maple syrup

$^1/_2$ cup apple juice

4 to 5 medium apples, peeled, cored, and sliced

2 tablespoons butter or margarine

$^1/_8$ teaspoon sea salt

4 to 5 medium sweet potatoes, boiled in their skins

$^1/_4$ cup finely chopped walnuts (optional)

Preheat oven to 400°F. Grease an 8 x 8-inch baking dish.

Place syrup and apple juice in saucepan. Add apples, butter or margarine, and a pinch of salt. Cook over low heat until apples are tender. Peel and place half of the sweet potatoes into a well-greased baking dish. Spoon half of the apple-syrup mixture over the sweet potatoes. Repeat with the remainder of the potatoes and apples. Top with nuts. Bake at 400°F for 20 minutes.

Makes 6 to 8 servings

Maple Carrots

3 cups peeled and diagonally sliced carrots

$1/4$ cup maple syrup

1 tablespoon safflower oil (optional)

Cook the carrots gently in a small amount of water. When tender crisp, add the maple syrup and, if desired, safflower oil. Simmer briefly and serve piping hot.

Makes 6 servings

Oatmeal Stuffing

1 lemon

1 ³/₄ cups rolled oats

1 tablespoon fresh thyme, chopped

2 tablespoons fresh parsley, chopped

Sea salt to taste

1 egg

2 tablespoons milk or other liquid

Preheat the oven to 325°F.

Grate the rind of the lemon and squeeze out 1 teaspoon of lemon juice. Set aside. Combine the oats with the thyme, parsley, lemon rind, and salt. Beat the egg with the milk and 1 teaspoon of lemon juice. Mix into the oat mixture, combining well. Stuff into fish, meat, or poultry or place in an oven-proof glass dish and bake for 30 minutes, until moist and tender.

Makes approximately 1 ³/₄ cups

Orange Vegetable Kabobs

I have always enjoyed making vegetable kabobs over our backyard grill. I would also serve BBQ chicken (or meat kabobs) and a nice big tossed salad. For this recipe, you can add or remove any vegetable or fruit you like. You can also change the marinade ingredients as you wish. The new food safety policy recommends cooking meat or poultry kabobs separately from the fruit and vegetable kabobs. This is to eliminate cross-contamination from the poultry and to make sure the meat or poultry is cooked to the proper temperature.

8 pineapple chunks

1 large navel orange, unpeeled

2 bananas, cut into 8 chunks

8 medium fresh mushrooms

8 cherry tomatoes

2 small yellow summer squash, cut into 1-inch chunks

MARINADE

$1/2$ cup oil

$1/3$ cup orange juice

2 tablespoons lemon juice

2 teaspoons sugar or honey

1 teaspoon sea salt, optional

$1/2$ teaspoon parsley, optional

$1/2$ teaspoon sage, optional

Cut the orange into eight wedges; halve each wedge. Alternately thread vegetables and fruit pieces onto eight metal or soaked wooden skewers. Place in a shallow oblong dish.

Prepare the marinade in a bowl. Whisk together the oil, orange juice, lemon juice, and sweetener, and seasonings if desired. Pour over skewers. Marinate for 15 minutes, turning and basting frequently. Grill, covered, over indirect heat for 10 to 15 minutes or until the vegetables are crisp-tender. Brush with marinade just before serving.

Makes 4 servings

Oriental Tomato Skillet

2 tablespoons allowed oil

2 medium unpeeled zucchini, sliced $^1/_4$-inch thick

3 medium tomatoes, cut into wedges

1 (4-ounce) can sliced mushrooms, drained

Sea salt to taste

$^1/_4$ teaspoon curry powder

$^1/_4$ teaspoon ginger

Heat the oil in a wok or skillet; add the zucchini. Stir-fry over medium heat for 5 minutes; stir in the remaining ingredients. Cook, covered, 5 minutes longer, or until the vegetables are tender but slightly crisp.

Makes 6 servings

Rice Pilaf

1 $\frac{3}{4}$ cups long-grain rice

$\frac{1}{3}$ cup dried, unsulfured apricots, chopped

$\frac{1}{3}$ cup seedless raisins

$\frac{1}{3}$ cup walnuts (optional), chopped

2 $\frac{1}{2}$ cups chicken broth (see page 193)

$\frac{1}{2}$ teaspoon nutmeg (optional)

Sea salt to taste

Put the rice, apricots, raisins, and walnuts into a pan and pour the chicken broth over it. Stir in the nutmeg and season with salt. Bring to a boil, stirring constantly. Lower the heat, cover, and simmer for 15 minutes, or until the rice is tender and the broth has been absorbed.

Makes 6 servings

Cranberry Relish

2 cups cranberries

$^{1}/_{2}$ cup sweet apple cider

$^{1}/_{4}$ cup honey

$^{1}/_{2}$ teaspoon ground allspice

Pinch of ground cloves

Blend all ingredients together. Store in container in refrigerator.

Makes 3 cups

14.

Main Courses

One of the biggest difficulties the family cook has is to create new, interesting, and appetizing meals every day. Food allergies make the challenge even greater but not impossible.

We took our favorite recipes, made a few substitutions, and created meals that most people don't even realize are allergy-free. Try them yourself.

BAKED CHICKEN WITH TOMATO RICE STUFFING ... 226

BROILED BURGERS ... 227

CHERRY AND ORANGE DUCK ... 228

CHICKEN CHOP SUEY ... 229

CHICKEN OR TURKEY LOAF ... 230

CHICKEN SUPREME ... 231

FISH AMANDINE ... 232

FLOUNDER FLORENTINE ... 233

HONEY BAKED CHICKEN ... 234

HONEY BAKED CORNISH HENS ... 235

LAMB PILAF ... 236

PINEAPPLE PORK CHOPS WITH RICE ... 237

PORK CHOP SPANISH RICE ... 238

QUICK SAVORY MEAT LOAF ... 239

SLOPPY JOES ... 240

Baked Chicken with Tomato Rice Stuffing

3 pounds chicken, cut up

2 tablespoons oil

$^1/_3$ cup chopped celery

$^2/_3$ cup uncooked rice

1 cup chopped tomatoes

$^1/_2$ cup water

$^3/_4$ teaspoon sea salt

$^1/_4$ teaspoon sage

Preheat the oven to 350°F.

   Brown the chicken in oil in a heavy skillet. While the chicken browns, combine the celery, rice, tomatoes, and water in a mixing bowl. Turn the mixture into an 11 x 7-inch baking dish. Arrange the chicken on the rice. Sprinkle with salt and sage. Cover and bake for 1 hour, or until the chicken is tender.

Makes 6 servings

Broiled Burgers

1 pound ground beef

$1/2$ teaspoon sea salt

$1/4$ cup pure tomato sauce (see page 307)

$1/4$ cup chopped mushrooms

$1/4$ cup finely chopped celery

$1/4$ cup finely chopped carrots

$1/4$ cup chopped sunflower seeds

4 thick slices tomato

Combine the ground beef, salt, tomato sauce, mushrooms, celery, carrots, and sunflower seeds. Shape into four patties. Broil to the desired doneness. Top each burger with a tomato slice before serving.

Makes 4 servings

Cherry and Orange Duck

This quick and easy recipe is a nice alternative to chicken or turkey.

1 orange
1 (4-pound) duck
Sea salt to taste
1 pound cherries
Rind of 1 orange, grated
Juice of 2 oranges
$^3/_4$ cup chicken broth (see page 193)

Preheat the oven to 400°F.

Peel the orange, cut in half, and place in the cavity of the duck. Put the duck on a rack in a roasting pan. Prick the skin all over with a fork to allow the fat to run out. Rub the skin with salt. Roast the duck for about 1 hour. Pit the cherries and put them in a bowl. Add the grated orange rind plus the orange juice. When the duck has cooked for an hour, drain off the fat that has collected in the roasting pan. Remove the rack and put the duck back in the pan. Pour the cherries and orange juice around the duck with the chicken broth. Cover the pan with foil and roast for 30 minutes more. Remove the duck to a warmed serving platter. Drain half of the cherries in the pan and put them around the duck and keep it warm.

For the sauce, put the remaining cherries into a blender or food processor with the cooking liquid and blend until smooth. Reheat the sauce, season to taste with salt, and serve with the duck.

Makes 8 servings

Chicken Chop Suey

1 cup chopped celery

$^1/_2$ cup diced carrots

$^1/_2$ cup sliced water chestnuts

1 cup sliced mushrooms

$2^1/_2$ tablespoons oil

2 cups chicken or pork, cooked and cut into 1-inch strips

2 cups chicken broth (see page 193)

2 tablespoons arrowroot

$^1/_4$ cup cold water

1 cup fresh sprouts (try mung beans)

In a wok or heavy-bottomed skillet, sauté the celery, carrots, water chestnuts, and mushrooms in oil until just tender. Add the chicken or pork and chicken broth, and simmer while stirring constantly. Dissolve the arrowroot in cold water and add gradually, stirring until it is cooked and the chop suey is thickened. Add raw bean sprouts just before serving.

Makes 6 servings

VARIATIONS, IF TOLERATED:
- In place of arrowroot, use 2 tablespoons cornstarch.

Chicken or Turkey Loaf

1 cup chicken broth (see page 193)

1 cup crushed rice crackers

2 tablespoons butter, melted, or oil

3 cups ground chicken or turkey

$^1/_2$ cup chopped celery

3 tablespoons finely chopped carrot (optional)

2 teaspoons sage

1 teaspoon sea salt

Preheat the oven to 325°F.

In a large bowl, mix all the ingredients together thoroughly and pat into a greased loaf pan. Bake for 1 hour, or until done.

Makes 6 servings

VARIATIONS, IF TOLERATED:
- Mix 2 eggs with the rest of the ingredients.
- Substitute wheat crackers for the rice crackers.
- Add $^1/_2$ cup tomato paste if you want a tomato flavor.

Chicken Supreme

3 medium-size chicken breasts, halved, or 6 chicken thighs

$^1/_2$ teaspoon sea salt

$^1/_2$ teaspoon sage

1$^3/_4$ cups chicken broth (see page 193)

MUSHROOM SAUCE

3 tablespoons oat flour

$^1/_4$ cup cold water

Reserved pan juices

1 (4-ounce) can sliced mushrooms, drained

Preheat the oven to 350°F.

Sprinkle the chicken with salt and sage. Place in an 11 x 7-inch baking dish. Pour the broth over the chicken. Cover with foil and bake for 30 minutes. Remove the foil and bake 45 minutes longer. Remove the chicken to a warm platter. Strain the pan juices and reserve for the mushroom sauce. For the Mushroom Sauce, blend the flour with cold water in a saucepan. Slowly stir in the reserved pan juices. Cook and stir over low heat until the sauce thickens and bubbles. Boil for 3 to 4 minutes longer, then add the mushrooms. Heat thoroughly. Spoon the sauce over the chicken.

Makes 6 servings

VARIATIONS, IF TOLERATED:
- **Substitute 2$^1/_2$ tablespoons cornstarch or wheat flour for the oat flour.**

Fish Amandine

1 $1/2$ teaspoons oil, such as almond oil

$1/2$ cup slivered or chopped almonds

1 $1/2$ pounds fish fillets

2 tablespoons lemon juice (optional)

In a small saucepan, heat the oil and sauté the nuts until lightly browned. Set the saucepan aside. Cook the fish in a nonstick frying pan until it is opaque and flakes easily with a fork. Return the almonds to the heat. Add the lemon juice and warm thoroughly. Pour over the fish.

Makes 4 servings

Flounder Florentine

$1/8$ teaspoon dill, crushed

2 tablespoons oil

$1 1/2$ pounds fresh spinach, chopped

$1/2$ cup cooked brown rice

$1/3$ cup chopped almonds, toasted

1 tablespoon lemon juice

6 flounder fillets (about $1 1/2$ pounds)

Preheat the oven to 350°F. Oil a shallow l0 x 6-inch baking dish. In a saucepan, combine the dill, oil, and spinach and sauté just enough to wilt the spinach. Add the rice, almonds, and lemon juice. Heat, stirring occasionally. Place $1/4$ cup of the mixture on each fish fillet. Roll up and press the ends securely. Arrange on a baking dish and bake for 20 minutes. If desired, serve with Mushroom Sauce (see page 231).

Makes 6 servings

Honey Baked Chicken

2 tablespoons oil

1 (3-pound) chicken, cut into serving-size pieces

1 teaspoon sea salt

$^1/_2$ teaspoon sage

$^1/_2$ teaspoon thyme

2 large apples, sliced

2 teaspoons honey

$^1/_4$ cup apple juice

Preheat the oven to 350°F.

Heat the oil in a large skillet. Sprinkle the chicken with seasonings and brown in hot oil on all sides. Transfer to an 11 x 7-inch baking dish. Place apple slices between the chicken pieces, drizzle with honey, and pour juice over all. Cover and bake for about 50 minutes, or until the chicken is tender. Serve hot.

Makes 6 servings

Honey Baked Cornish Hens

*As you can see, this is the same recipe as the Honey Baked Chicken.
I just wanted to show you how easily you can change ingredients.*

2 tablespoons oil

3 cornish hens, halved

1 teaspoon sea salt

$1/2$ teaspoon sage

2 large pears, sliced

2 teaspoons honey

$1/4$ cup pear juice

Preheat the oven to 350°F.

I leat the oil in a large skillet. Sprinkle the cornish hen with seasonings and brown in hot oil on all sides. Transfer to an 11 x 7-inch baking dish. Place pear slices between the cornish hen pieces, drizzle with honey, and pour juice over all. Cover and bake for about 40 minutes, or until the cornish hen is tender. Serve hot.

Makes 6 servings

Lamb Pilaf

3 pounds lamb stew meat

6 cups lamb stock or water

1 teaspoon basil

1 teaspoon oregano

1 teaspoon rosemary

1 teaspoon sea salt

$1/2$ cup chopped celery

$1 1/2$ cups uncooked brown rice

$1/2$ cup slivered almonds

3 tablespoons oil

$2/3$ cup raisins

Cut the lamb into $1 1/2$-inch cubes, trimming away fat. Simmer lamb bones, if desired, for 1 to 2 hours to make stock. Put the lamb, stock or water, seasonings, and half the celery into a pot and simmer for 1 hour, or until the lamb is tender. Lift out the lamb and set aside. Strain the stock. To the empty pan, add the brown rice and 4 cups strained stock, stir, and cover tightly. Simmer over medium heat until the stock is absorbed and the rice is tender, about 40 minutes. The last 10 to 15 minutes, add the remaining celery. Mix the lamb and rice together gently and serve.

Sauté the almonds lightly in oil until golden and remove with a slotted spoon. Then sauté the raisins in the same pan with more oil, if necessary, until they are puffy. Scatter both over the lamb and rice.

Makes 6 to 8 servings

Pineapple Pork Chops with Rice

4 pork chops, $^1/_2$ inch to $^3/_4$ inch thick

Sea salt to taste

1 (8-ounce) can unsweetened crushed pineapple

1 cup water or pineapple juice

$^3/_4$ teaspoon sea salt

1 $^1/_2$ cups cooked rice

Sprinkle the pork chops with salt. In a large skillet over medium-high heat, brown the pork chops on both sides. Add the pineapple and reduce the heat to low. Cover and simmer until tender, about 30 minutes. Move the chops to the side of the pan. Add the water and salt. Bring to a full boil and stir in the rice. Remove from the heat. Cover and let stand for 5 minutes.

Makes 4 servings

Pork Chop Spanish Rice

6 pork chops, $^1/_2$ inch thick

1 $^1/_2$ teaspoons sea salt

$^3/_4$ cup long-grain rice

$^1/_2$ teaspoon sugar

3 $^1/_2$ cups canned whole tomatoes with juice

Brown the pork chops. Drain off excess fat. Sprinkle the salt over the meat. Add the rice. Mix the sugar with the tomatoes, and pour over the meat and rice. Cover and cook over low heat for 45 minutes to 1 hour, spooning the liquid over the rice occasionally.

Makes 6 servings

Quick Savory Meat Loaf

2 pounds ground beef

$^1/_3$ cup Minute Tapioca

1 $^1/_2$ teaspoons sea salt

$^1/_4$ teaspoon savory (optional)

1 (12-ounce) can tomatoes, broken up

Preheat the oven to 350°F.

In a large bowl, combine all the ingredients. Mix well. Spoon into a 9 x 5-inch loaf pan. Press in lightly. Bake for 1 to 1 $^3/_4$ hours.

Makes 8 servings

Sloppy Joes

1 $\frac{1}{2}$ pounds ground beef

3 tablespoons apple cider vinegar

$\frac{1}{4}$ cup unsweetened pineapple juice

3 tablespoons maple sugar

1 cup tomato sauce (see page 307)

$\frac{1}{2}$ cup water

$\frac{1}{2}$ cup chopped mushrooms (optional)

$\frac{1}{4}$ cup finely chopped celery (optional)

Sea salt to taste

Brown the ground beef in a skillet. Drain off excess fat. Add the remaining ingredients. Cover and simmer for 20 minutes. Taste for sweetness and seasoning. Serve on allowed bread or buns.

Makes 6 sandwiches

VARIATIONS, IF TOLERATED:
- Substitute an equal amount of sugar for the maple sugar.
- Substitute 1 tablespoon lemon juice for the pineapple juice.

15.

Cookies, Bars, Fruit Treats, and Snacks

When my children were younger, I would try to have a nutritious snack ready for them when they came home from school. Let your children look forward to some of these special goodies.

COOKIES AND BARS

ALMOND COOKIES ... 244

ALMOND CRESCENTS ... 245

APPLESAUCE COOKIES ... 246

BANANA OATMEAL COOKIES ... 247

BARLEY DROP COOKIES ... 248

BLUEBERRY DELIGHT COOKIES ... 249

BROWNIES . . . 250

BUTTERSCOTCH COOKIES ... 251

CHOCOLATE CRUNCH NUT BUTTER BARS ... 252

HONEY NUT RAISIN COOKIES ... 253

MAPLE OATMEAL COOKIES ... 254

NUT BUTTER GRANOLA BARS ... 255

PECAN BALLS ... 256

RAISIN NUT COOKIES ... 257

FRUIT TREATS

APPLE CRISP ... 258

APPLE RICE BETTY ... 259

APPLESAUCE ... 260

BAKED PEARS ... 260

CANTALOUPE SHERBET ... 261

FRENCH-FRIED BANANAS ... 261

FROSTY FREEZER TREATS ... 262

FRUIT SHERBET ... 263

JAMAICAN BAKED BANANAS ... 264

PINEAPPLE PORCUPINES ... 265

SCALLOPED APPLES ... 266

WATERMELON SHERBET ... 267

SNACKS

APPLE SNACK ... 268

CAROB CANDY ... 269

COCONUT-COVERED RAISINS ... 270

QUICK BANANA OATMEAL CRISP ... 271

Almond Cookies

2 cups almonds

$^1/_2$ cup honey

$^1/_2$ teaspoon sea salt

$^1/_4$ cup water

3 tablespoons carob powder (optional)

1 tablespoon honey

1 teaspoon water

24 whole almonds

Preheat the oven to 350°F. Grease a cookie sheet.

Grind the 2 cups nuts in a blender, being careful not to overgrind. Turn into a small bowl; combine with honey, salt, water, and carob powder, if using. Drop by the teaspoonful 2 inches apart onto a greased cookie sheet. Make a glaze of
1 tablespoon honey and 1 teaspoon water and brush over cookies. Place whole almonds on top of each cookie for decoration. Bake for 10 to 12 minutes.

Makes 24 cookies

Almond Crescents

1 $^{1}/_{3}$ cups potato starch

$^{1}/_{3}$ cup maple sugar

$^{1}/_{4}$ teaspoon sea salt

2 teaspoons baking powder

$^{1}/_{4}$ cup butter or margarine

$^{1}/_{3}$ cup almond milk or water

$^{1}/_{2}$ teaspoon vanilla

$^{1}/_{2}$ cup shredded coconut or crushed almonds

Preheat the oven to 350°F. Grease a cookie sheet.

   Place the dry ingredients in a bowl and cut in the butter. Add the almond milk and vanilla, working the dough into a soft, smooth consistency that holds together without being sticky. Add coconut or almonds. Form into small crescents and place 2 inches apart on the cookie sheet. Bake for 12 to 15 minutes.

Makes 24 cookies

VARIATIONS, IF TOLERATED:

- Substitute 2 cups wheat flour for the potato starch.
- Substitute an equal amount of milk for the nut milk.
- Roll in powdered sugar.

Applesauce Cookies

$1/4$ cup butter or margarine

$1/2$ cup maple syrup

$1/3$ cup thick applesauce, unsweetened

$1/4$ teaspoon vanilla

1 cup potato starch

$1/4$ teaspoon sea salt

2 teaspoons baking powder

$1/4$ cup chopped nuts (optional)

Preheat the oven to 350°F. Grease a cookie sheet.

In a large bowl, cream the butter and sugar or syrup together. Add the applesauce and vanilla. Sift together the dry ingredients and stir into the maple mixture. Add the nuts. Drop by the teaspoonful 2 inches apart onto a greased cookie sheet. Bake for about 12 minutes.

Makes 24 cookies

VARIATIONS, IF TOLERATED:
- Substitute an equal amount of sugar for the maple sugar.
- Substitute $1 1/2$ cups wheat flour for the potato starch.

Banana Oatmeal Cookies

$^1/_2$ cup maple sugar, maple syrup, or sugar

$^3/_4$ cup butter or margarine

1 cup oat flour

1 $^1/_3$ cups mashed ripe bananas

3 cups rolled oats

1 cup raisins OR $^1/_2$ cup raisins

   and $^1/_2$ cup chopped nuts (optional)

Preheat the oven to 325°F. Grease a cookie sheet.

In a large bowl, cream together the sugar and butter. Mix in the flour. Stir in the bananas. Add the rolled oats and raisins and mix well. Drop by the teaspoonful 2 inches apart onto a greased cookie sheet. Bake for 20 minutes.

Makes 72 cookies

VARIATIONS, IF TOLERATED:
- Substitute 1 cup wheat flour for 1 cup oat flour.
- Add 1 egg to the creamed sugar and butter.

Barley Drop Cookies

$1/3$ cup butter or margarine

$3/4$ cup sugar

$1 1/2$ teaspoons pure vanilla

2 cups barley flour

1 tablespoon baking powder

$1/2$ teaspoon sea salt

$1/2$ cup water, nut milk, or goat's milk

$1/2$ cup dried blueberries, cranberries, or raisins (optional)

$1/2$ cup chopped nuts (optional)

Preheat the oven to 350°F. Grease a cookie sheet.

In a large bowl, cream the butter and sugar and stir in the vanilla. In a small bowl, combine the dry ingredients together. Mix the dry ingredients alternately with $1/2$ cup liquid. Blend well. Add dried fruits and nuts, if desired. Drop by the teaspoonful onto a greased cookie sheet and bake for 12 to 14 minutes.

Makes about 56 cookies

Blueberry Delight Cookies

$\frac{1}{3}$ cup butter or margarine

$\frac{2}{3}$ cup maple sugar

1 tablespoon coconut milk, water, or apple juice

1 teaspoon vanilla

$\frac{1}{4}$ teaspoon sea salt

$\frac{1}{2}$ teaspoon baking powder

1 cup rice flour

$\frac{1}{4}$ cup applesauce, unsweetened

$\frac{1}{4}$ cup fresh blueberries

Preheat the oven to 350°F. Grease a cookie sheet.

In a large bowl, cream the butter and sugar until fluffy. Add the coconut milk and vanilla and beat until smooth. Beat in all the other ingredients except the blueberries. Gently fold in the berries by hand. Drop by the teaspoonful 2 inches apart onto a greased cookie sheet. Bake 10 to 14 minutes.

Makes 48 cookies

VARIATIONS, IF TOLERATED:
- Substitute 1$\frac{3}{4}$ cups wheat flour for the rice flour.
- Add 1 egg to the creamed sugar and butter and omit the applesauce.
- Substitute an equal amount of milk for the coconut milk.

Brownies

2 ounces (squares) unsweetened chocolate

$1/3$ cup butter or margarine

2 eggs

$1/2$ teaspoon sea salt

1 cup sugar

1 cup rice flour

1 teaspoon xanthan gum

$1/2$ teaspoon vanilla

$1/2$ cup chopped walnuts (optional)

Preheat the oven to 350°F. Grease an 8-inch-square pan.

Melt the chocolate and butter over hot water. Set aside to cool. Beat the eggs until foamy. Add salt and beat until thick. Add the sugar gradually and continue beating until pale yellow. Blend in the cooled chocolate and butter mixture. Add the flour, xanthan gum, vanilla, and nuts. Stir until smooth. Spread into the greased pan. Bake for 35 to 40 minutes. Cool slightly and cut into squares.

Makes about 9 brownies

VARIATIONS, IF TOLERATED:
- Substitute 1$3/4$ cups wheat flour for the rice flour.

Butterscotch Cookies

$1/3$ cup butter or margarine

$1/3$ cup honey or sugar

1 teaspoon vanilla

$1/4$ teaspoon sea salt

$1/2$ teaspoon baking powder

1 cup rolled oats

$1/4$ cup oat flour

$1/2$ cup finely chopped almonds (optional)

Preheat the oven to 350°F. Grease a cookie sheet.

In a large bowl, cream the butter and honey until fluffy. Add the vanilla and beat until smooth. Beat in all the other ingredients. Drop by the teaspoonful 3 inches apart onto a well-greased cookie sheet. Bake for 8 to 10 minutes or until light brown. Let cool completely before removing from the sheet.

Makes 36 cookies

VARIATIONS, IF TOLERATED:
- Use $1/2$ cup wheat flour and $3/4$ cup rolled oats in place of the 1 cup rolled oats and $1/4$ cup oat flour.
- Add 1 egg to the creamed butter and honey.

Chocolate Crunch Nut Butter Bars

$^1/_3$ cup butter

$^1/_2$ cup creamy nut butter

$^1/_2$ cup brown sugar

$^1/_2$ cup honey

1 to 1$^1/_2$ cups crushed salted nuts (optional)

2 cups Rice Krispies

1 cup semi-sweet chocolate chips

$^1/_2$ cup creamy nut butter

In saucepan, combine butter, nut butter, brown sugar, and honey. Stir over low heat, until well blended. Add nuts and cereal; stir. Pour mixture into greased 9 x 9-inch pan; cool. In double boiler, melt chocolate chips and nut butter. Pour warm chocolate mixture over cooled cereal mixture. Chill in refrigerator overnight. Cut into squares and serve.

Makes 20 to 24 bars

Honey Nut Raisin Cookies

$^3/_4$ cup honey

$^2/_3$ cup oil

2 eggs, beaten

1 teaspoon vanilla extract

1 cup chopped pecans

1 cup raisins, plumped

$2^1/_4$ cups barley flour

Preheat the oven to 350°F.

Blend all the ingredients together, using only enough barley flour to make the dough a good consistency to drop by teaspoonfuls onto greased cookie sheets. Bake for 12 to 15 minutes.

Makes 5 dozen cookies

Maple Oatmeal Cookies

1 cup oat flour

$^1/_2$ teaspoon sea salt

1 teaspoon baking powder

1 cup rolled oats

$^1/_2$ cup chopped walnuts (optional)

$^1/_2$ cup butter or margarine

1 egg or egg replacer

$^3/_4$ cup sugar

1 $^1/_2$ teaspoons vanilla

Preheat the oven to 400°F. Grease a cookie sheet.

Sift together the oat flour, salt, and baking powder. Add the oats and chopped walnuts. Mix well and set aside. Cream the butter with the egg. Add the sugar and vanilla and mix well. Combine all the ingredients. Drop by the teaspoonful 2 inches apart onto a greased cookie sheet. Bake for 8 to 12 minutes.

Makes 72 cookies

VARIATIONS, IF TOLERATED:
- Substitute 1 cup wheat flour for the oat flour.

Nut Butter Granola Bars

2 tablespoons oil

1 cup rolled oats

1 cup mixed nuts (optional)

$^1/_3$ cup grated unsweetened coconut

$^1/_4$ teaspoon sea salt

1 cup nut butter

$^3/_4$ cup honey or sugar

$^3/_4$ cup fruit juice, water, nut milk, or goat's milk

1 teaspoon pure vanilla

1 teaspoon xanthan gum (optional)

1 small ripe banana, mashed

Preheat the oven to 325°F. Grease a 9 x13-inch pan.

Heat the oil in a large saucepan. Add the oats, nuts, coconut, and salt. Toast lightly over medium heat, stirring constantly. In a small mixing bowl, combine the nut butter, honey, juice, vanilla, xanthan gum, and banana. Add to the oat and nut mixture. Cook for about 5 minutes, stirring constantly. Spread the mixture in the greased pan and bake for 25 to 30 minutes. Cool and cut into bars.

Makes 15 bars

VARIATIONS, IF TOLERATED:
- Use $^1/_2$ cup wheat flour and $^3/_4$ cup rolled oats in place of the 1 cup rolled oats.
- Add 1 egg to the nut butter mixture and omit the xanthan gum.

Pecan Balls

$1/3$ cup butter or margarine

$1/3$ cup sugar

1 tablespoon water or nut milk

1 teaspoon vanilla

$1/4$ teaspoon sea salt

$1/2$ teaspoon baking powder

1 cup rice flour

$1/4$ cup pecans or coconut, finely chopped

Preheat the oven to 350°F.

Mix together all the ingredients and form by hand into balls. Place on ungreased cookie sheets 1 inch apart. Bake for 8 to 10 minutes.

Makes 36 cookies

VARIATIONS, IF TOLERATED:
- Roll cookies into powdered sugar (which contains corn), just after they are baked.

Raisin Nut Cookies

$1/3$ cup butter or margarine

$1/2$ cup honey or maple syrup, or $2/3$ cup maple sugar,
   or $2/3$ cup sugar

1 teaspoon vanilla

$3/4$ cup rice flour

$1/2$ cup potato starch flour

$1/4$ teaspoon sea salt

$1/2$ teaspoon baking soda

$1/4$ to $1/2$ cup raisins

$1/4$ to $1/2$ cup chopped nuts (optional)

Preheat the oven to 375°F.

In a large bowl, cream the butter, honey, and vanilla. Sift the dry ingredients together and add to the honey mixture. Mix well. Stir in the raisins and nuts. Drop by the teaspoonful 2 inches apart onto an ungreased cookie sheet. Bake for 10 to 12 minutes.

Makes 48 cookies

VARIATIONS, IF TOLERATED:
* Use 1 cup wheat flour in place of the other flours.

Apple Crisp

3 cups peeled, sliced, or chopped apples

1 tablespoon oat or rice flour

2 tablespoons maple syrup or honey

1 teaspoon nutmeg (optional)

$1/8$ teaspoon sea salt

1 tablespoon water

$1/2$ cup rolled oats

$1/4$ teaspoon sea salt

$1/4$ cup butter or margarine

$1/3$ cup maple sugar or regular sugar

Preheat the oven to 375°F. Grease an 8-inch-square casserole dish.

Combine the apples, flour, maple syrup, nutmeg, salt, and water. Put into the casserole dish. Mix together the oats, salt, butter, and maple sugar. Sprinkle on top of the apple mixture. Bake for 35 to 45 minutes.

Makes 8 servings

VARIATIONS, IF TOLERATED:
- Add $1/4$ cup nut butter to the topping and reduce the butter to 2 tablespoons.

Apple Rice Betty

1 cup honey or sugar

$^1/_4$ teaspoon cloves (optional)

$^1/_4$ teaspoon nutmeg (optional)

$^1/_4$ teaspoon sea salt

1 cup rice, cooked

4 large tart apples, peeled, cored, and thinly sliced

$^1/_2$ cup chopped walnuts (optional)

$^1/_4$ cup oil

Preheat the oven to 350°F. Grease an 11 x 7-inch baking dish.

Mix the honey with the spices and salt. Place a thin layer of rice in the baking dish. Add a layer of thinly sliced apples and sprinkle with the honey, spices, and nuts. Repeat the layers until all the ingredients are used (ending with honey and nuts on top). Pour oil over all. Bake until the apples are soft. Serve hot.

Makes 10 servings

Applesauce

4 medium apples
$^1/_2$ cup honey or maple syrup
2 tablespoons pineapple, apple, or pear juice

Wash and core the apples and cut into small pieces. Place all the ingredients in a blender or food processor and process to the desired texture. No cooking is necessary.

Makes 4 servings

Baked Pears

This is an elegant and quick dessert that takes minutes to prepare and only fifteen to twenty minutes to cook!

4 pears
$^1/_4$ to $^1/_2$ cup maple syrup or honey

Preheat the oven to 350°F.

Pare, halve, and core the pears. Arrange in a greased baking dish, drizzle with maple syrup or honey, and bake 15 to 20 minutes, or until the pears are tender.

Makes 4 servings

Cantaloupe Sherbet

1 $\frac{1}{2}$ cups water

$\frac{1}{2}$ cup honey or sugar

3 cups fresh cantaloupe pulp and juice

Boil the water and honey together for about 5 minutes, until the honey dissolves. Put the cantaloupe pulp and juice in a blender and puree well. Add honey and water mixture and blend well. Pour into ice cube trays. Freeze until firm.

Makes 6 servings

French-Fried Bananas

4 medium green bananas

$\frac{1}{3}$ cup allowed oil

$\frac{1}{2}$ teaspoon sea salt

Peel the bananas and cut in halves crosswise. Cut each half into six strips. Heat the oil in a 10-inch skillet over medium heat. Add a single layer of banana strips and fry until the edges are golden brown. Remove with a slotted spoon and drain on paper towels. Repeat with the remaining banana strips. Sprinkle lightly with salt. Serve at once.

Makes 4 servings

Frosty Freezer Treats

When they were young, my kids loved making these frozen bananas—they're quite messy and gooey and they loved eating them. They taste like banana ice cream.

2 medium bananas, peeled
$^1/_2$ cup pure nut butter
$^1/_4$ cup nut milk or milk
2 tablespoons honey
$^1/_2$ cup chopped nuts, toasted (optional)

Cut the bananas into halves or thirds crosswise and insert popsicle sticks into the ends. Place on a cookie sheet and freeze. Blend the nut butter with the nut milk and honey until smooth. Coat the frozen banana pieces with the nut butter mixture and roll in almonds to cover. Return to the freezer to harden. Wrap in plastic wrap before storing in freezer.

> **Note: you might want to double the batch.**

Makes 4 to 6 fruit treats

Fruit Sherbet

²/₃ cup tapioca flour

²/₃ cup honey

3 cups water

1 quart blueberries or strawberries, sliced

1 teaspoon vanilla

Mix the tapioca flour, honey, and water in a small saucepan and bring to a boil. Cook over medium heat, stirring constantly, until thick. Remove from the heat and stir in the fruit and vanilla. Puree in a blender until smooth. Pour into freezer trays. Freeze until firm.

Makes 2 quarts

Jamaican Baked Bananas

4 to 6 bananas (sliced if desired)

2 tablespoons butter or margarine

2 tablespoons maple sugar

$^7/_8$ cup pineapple or apple juice

2 tablespoons tapioca flour

2 tablespoons pineapple or apple juice

$^1/_4$ to $^1/_2$ cup raisins, dried blueberries, or dried cranberries

Grated coconut

Preheat the oven to 350°F.

Peel the bananas and arrange in an 8-inch-square casserole dish. Combine the butter, sugar, and juice in a saucepan, bring to a boil, and cook, stirring constantly. Combine the tapioca flour with 2 tablespoons juice and add to the hot mixture. Cook until clear and thick. Add raisins or dried fruit. Pour over the bananas. Top with grated coconut. Bake for 25 to 30 minutes.

Makes 4 to 5 servings

VARIATIONS, IF TOLERATED:
- Substitute wheat flour for the tapioca flour.

Pineapple Porcupines

Save a thick cantaloupe shell. Place, cut side down, on a plate and stick the pineapple pieces into it using party toothpicks. The ingredients may be served as a "do-it-yourself" snack.

1 whole fresh pineapple

1 cup honey

1 cup sunflower or sesame seeds or coconut, chopped

Pare and core the pineapple. Cut it into pieces about 2 inches square. Insert a toothpick into each square. In a saucepan, warm the honey but do not boil. Dip the pineapple squares into the honey and roll them in seeds. If desired, put them in the freezer to harden.

Makes 8 to 9 servings

Scalloped Apples

6 large apples

$1/4$ teaspoon nutmeg

$1/4$ teaspoon sea salt

1 tablespoon lemon juice

$1/4$ cup water or apple juice

$3/4$ cup brown sugar

$1/4$ cup flour or oats

$1/3$ cup butter

Preheat oven to 400°F. Grease an 8 x 8-inch casserole dish.

Pare, core, and slice the apples. Place apples in the buttered casserole dish and sprinkle the nutmeg, salt, lemon juice, and liquid over the apples. Work the sugar, flour, and butter together until crumb-like in consistency. Spread this over the apples and bake for 30 minutes. This goes well with pork dishes.

Makes 6 servings

Watermelon Sherbet

2 to 4 cups watermelon, cubed, with seeds removed

$^1/_2$ to 1 tablespoon honey

Put the watermelon in a blender and puree well. Add a little honey if desired. Pour into ice cube trays or pint jars and freeze.

Makes 4 servings

VARIATIONS, IF TOLERATED:

- Substitute an equal amount of sugar for the honey.

Apple Snack

Apples will turn dark brown since they have no sulfuring agent, but taste just as flavorful.

2 pounds apples

Preheat the oven to 225°F.

Peel, core, and halve the apples. Shred coarsely and put on a buttered cookie sheet. Bake until dry. Remove from the cookie sheet with a pancake turner. Break into pieces. Store in an airtight container.

Makes 2 cups

Carob Candy

Have everything ready before you begin. The candy hardens fast!

1 cup honey or sugar

$1/3$ cup carob powder

Dash of sea salt

2 tablespoons butter or margarine

2 teaspoons vanilla

$1/2$ cup nut butter

3 cups rolled oats

In a large pan, mix the honey, carob powder, salt, and butter and boil for 1 minute.

Remove from the heat and add the vanilla, nut butter, and oats. Stir quickly and drop by the teaspoonful onto waxed paper to cool.

Makes 72 pieces

Coconut-Covered Raisins

$^1/_2$ cup honey

4 cups raisins

1 cup unsweetened coconut, toasted and finely grated

In a medium-size pan, warm the honey and stir in the raisins. Lift them out with a slotted spoon and drop into the coconut. Mix until well coated and spread on waxed paper. Separate and cool.

Makes 5 cups

Quick Banana Oatmeal Crisp

2 to 3 cups rolled oats

4 medium bananas

$1/4$ cup honey

Preheat the oven to 250°F.

Cover a nonstick cookie sheet with a thin layer of oats. Blend or mash the bananas and honey thoroughly. Drizzle the mixture over the oats and bake until leathery (about 1 hour). Cool, then tear apart.

Makes 2 to 3 servings

16.

Cakes, Pies,
and Puddings

For special occasions, we have created some unusual and delicious pies and cakes.

Try Pumpkin Pecan Pie for Thanksgiving or serve Banana Cake at a birthday party. Of course, you don't have to wait until a holiday to try these recipes.

CAKES

BANANA CAKE ... 275

BUTTERSCOTCH CHIFFON TUBE CAKE ... 276

CHIFFON "POUND" CAKE ... 277

FRUITY SPICE CAKE ... 278

OATMEAL-RAISIN CARROT CAKE ... 279

QUICK CHOCOLATE CAKE ... 280

RICE SPICE CAKE ... 281

TAPIOCA PINEAPPLE CAKE ... 282

FROSTINGS

BLENDER BROILED FROSTING ... 283

CONFETTI ICING ... 284

HONEY BUTTER FROSTING ... 285

MAPLE FROSTING ... 285

PIES

OATMEAL PIE SHELL ... 286

OLD-FASHIONED CHOCOLATE PIE ... 287

PEACH PIE WITH ALMOND CRUST ... 288

PUMPKIN PECAN PIE ... 289

RICE OR RYE PIE CRUST ... 290

STRAWBERRY PIE ... 291

PUDDINGS

APPLE TAPIOCA ... 292

APPLE TAPIOCA SUPREME ... 293

FRUITY RICE PUDDING ... 294

HASTY PUDDING ... 295

VANILLA PUDDING ... 296

RICE BROWN BETTY ... 297

RICE PUDDING ... 298

Banana Cake

2 cups oat flour

$^1/_2$ teaspoon sea salt

2 teaspoons baking powder

2 teaspoons safflower oil

$^1/_2$ cup banana, mashed

$^1/_2$ cup maple syrup, honey, or sugar

2 eggs or egg replacer

3 tablespoons cold water

Preheat the oven to 350°F. Grease an 8-inch-square pan.

Mix together the flour, salt, and baking powder. Add the oil, banana, syrup, eggs, and water. Mix well. Turn into the baking dish and bake for 25 to 30 minutes.

Makes 6 servings

VARIATIONS, IF TOLERATED:
- Substitute an equal amount of milk for the water.
- Substitute 1$^3/_4$ cups wheat flour for the oat flour.

Butterscotch Chiffon Tube Cake

1 $^3/_4$ cups barley flour

$^1/_2$ cup tapioca flour

4 teaspoons baking powder

1 teaspoon sea salt

$^1/_2$ cup vegetable oil

5 medium egg yolks

$^1/_2$ cup cold water

2 teaspoons vanilla extract

$^3/_4$ cup maple syrup or honey

1 cup egg whites (7 or 8 eggs)

$^1/_2$ teaspoon cream of tartar

Preheat the oven to 325°F.

Into a medium-size bowl, sift together the flours, baking powder, and salt. Form a well in the center. Combine the oil, egg yolks, water, vanilla, and maple syrup or honey. Add to the well in the dry ingredients. Beat with a spoon until smooth. In a large bowl, beat the egg whites with the cream of tartar until very stiff. Pour the batter gradually over the beaten egg whites and gently fold into the egg whites. *Do not stir.* Pour at once into an ungreased 10-inch tube pan. Bake for 65 to 70 minutes, or until the top springs back when lightly touched. Invert on a funnel until the cake has cooled.

Makes 10 to 12 servings

Chiffon "Pound" Cake

1$^1/_2$ cups rice flour

6 teaspoons baking powder

1 teaspoon sea salt

$^1/_2$ cup oil

$^3/_4$ cup maple syrup or honey or sugar

6 egg yolks, beaten

$^1/_4$ cup water or coconut milk

1 teaspoon vanilla

6 egg whites

$^1/_2$ teaspoon cream of tartar

Preheat the oven to 350°F.

Mix together the flour, baking powder, and salt. Add the oil, syrup, egg yolks, water, and vanilla. Beat until smooth. Beat the egg whites with cream of tartar until stiff but not dry. Fold into the batter. Pour into an ungreased 13 x 9-inch pan or tube pan. Bake for 35 minutes, until firm to the touch. Invert the pan on a rack to cool.

Makes 10 to 12 servings

VARIATIONS, IF TOLERATED:
- Add fruit topping if desired.
- Substitute an equal amount of milk for the water or coconut milk.

Fruity Spice Cake

1 cup water

2 cups raisins

1 cup maple sugar or sugar

$^1/_2$ cup butter or margarine

$^1/_2$ teaspoon nutmeg

$^1/_2$ teaspoon allspice

$^1/_2$ teaspoon sea salt

$1^1/_2$ cups potato starch or rice flour

2 teaspoons baking powder

1 teaspoon baking soda

1 cup chopped pecans (optional)

Preheat the oven to 375°F. Grease a 9-inch-square pan.

In a medium-size saucepan, bring the water, raisins, sugar, butter, spices, and salt to a boil. Simmer, uncovered, for 3 minutes. Let cool. Sift together the flour, baking powder, and baking soda. Stir in the raisin mixture and nuts. Beat until smooth. Pour into the baking dish and bake for 35 to 40 minutes. Cool in pan for 15 minutes. Turn out of pan and cool completely.

Makes 6 servings

> **VARIATIONS, IF TOLERATED:**
> - Substitute an equal amount of milk for the water.
> - Substitute 2 cups wheat flour for the rice flour.
> - Add 1 egg to the cooled raisin-butter mixture.

Oatmeal-Raisin Carrot Cake

1 cup honey

1 cup water or nut milk or goat's milk

$^1/_3$ cup butter or margarine

$^1/_2$ cup raisins

1 cup carrots, grated

$^1/_2$ teaspoon nutmeg (optional)

1 teaspoon ginger (optional)

1 teaspoon baking soda

1 teaspoon sea salt

2 teaspoons water

$2^1/_2$ cups oat flour or $1^3/_4$ cups rice flour

$2^1/_2$ teaspoons baking powder

$^1/_2$ cup chopped nuts (optional)

Preheat the oven to 350°F. Grease an 8 x 4-inch loaf pan.

Mix the honey, water, butter, raisins, carrots, and spices in a saucepan. Bring to a boil and simmer for 3 minutes. Cool to lukewarm. Mix together the baking soda, salt, and water and add to the honey mixture. Mix the flour and baking powder together and stir in. Fold in the nuts. Pour into the loaf pan and bake for 50 minutes.

Makes 6 servings

VARIATIONS, IF TOLERATED: *continued on next page*
- Substitute an equal amount of sugar for the honey.

Quick Chocolate Cake

1$^1/_2$ cups rice flour

2 heaping tablespoons carob powder or cocoa

$^1/_4$ teaspoon sea salt

1 teaspoon baking soda

1 cup maple sugar or sugar

$^1/_2$ cup safflower oil

1 teaspoon vanilla

1 cup warm water, nut milk, or goat's milk

Preheat the oven to 350°F.

Sift together the flour, carob powder, salt, baking soda, and sugar. Heap the dry ingredients into an ungreased 9-inch-square pan. In a 2-cup measuring cup, mix together the oil, vanilla, and water. Make a well in the center of the flour mixture, gently pour in the liquid, and mix. Bake for 40 minutes.

Makes 9 to 10 servings

VARIATIONS, IF TOLERATED:
- Substitute an equal amount of milk for the water or nut milk.
- Substitute 2 cups wheat flour for the rice flour.

Rice Spice Cake

1 cup honey or sugar

$^3/_4$ cup water

$^1/_3$ cup butter or margarine or oil

1 cup raisins

$^1/_2$ teaspoon sea salt

$^1/_2$ teaspoon ginger

$^1/_2$ teaspoon nutmeg

2$^1/_4$ cups rice flour, sifted

1$^1/_2$ teaspoons baking powder

Preheat the oven to 325°F. Grease an 8 x 4-inch loaf pan.

Combine the first five ingredients in a medium-size saucepan, bring to a boil, reduce the heat, and simmer for 3 minutes, stirring constantly. Remove from the heat. Sift together the spices, flour, and baking powder. Add to the raisin mixture and beat well. Pour into the loaf pan and bake for 1 hour.

Makes 8 to 9 servings

VARIATIONS, IF TOLERATED:
- Substitute an equal amount of milk for the water.
- Substitute 2$^3/_4$ cups wheat flour for the rice flour.
- Add 1 egg to the cooled raisin-butter mixture.

Tapioca Pineapple Cake

---

1 $^3/_4$ cups tapioca flour

$^1/_2$ teaspoon baking powder

$^1/_2$ teaspoon sea salt

$^1/_2$ to 1 cup honey or sugar

$^1/_2$ cup safflower oil

$^1/_4$ cups crushed pineapple, drained (reserve liquid)

1 tablespoon vanilla

Preheat the oven to 350°F. Grease and flour (with tapioca flour) two 8-inch cake pans.

Mix together the dry ingredients. Combine the honey, safflower oil, drained pineapple, and vanilla and mix well. Add the liquid ingredients to the dry ingredients. Add the pineapple liquid and extra water as needed to bring to the consistency of cake batter. Pour into prepared cake pans and bake for 25 to 35 minutes. Cool. Frost with Blender Broiled Frosting (see opposite page), if desired.

Makes 8 to 9 servings

VARIATIONS, IF TOLERATED:
- Substitute 1 $^3/_4$ cups wheat flour for the tapioca flour.
- Add 1 egg to the pineapple liquid.

Blender Broiled Frosting

1 cup honey

$^1/_2$ cup safflower oil

1 teaspoon vanilla

2 cups unsweetened coconut, shredded

Combine the first three ingredients in a blender. Pour into a mixing bowl and add the coconut. Stir until well mixed. Spread on cake and broil until bubbly, approximately 4 to 5 minutes.

> **Note:** Chopped mixed nuts and/or seeds may be substituted for some or all of the coconut.

Makes 3 cups

Confetti Icing

$^3/_4$ cup unsweetened coconut, shredded

Natural food coloring

1$^1/_2$ cups honey

$^3/_4$ cup water

Color the coconut to a desired shade using natural food coloring. Set aside. Cut the cake up into serving slices or squares. Mix the honey and water together to get a thin, slightly sticky consistency. Drizzle the honey and water mixture over the cake slices and then sprinkle with confetti coconut. The effect is beautiful and the taste is delightfully sweet and moist.

Makes 3 cups

Honey Butter Frosting

$^1/_4$ cup honey

$^1/_4$ cup butter or margarine

2 cups sifted confectioners' sugar OR 1 to 2 cups tapioca flour

1 teaspoon water or milk

Beat the honey and butter together. Add the sugar and water and adjust to the right consistency.

Makes 2$^1/_2$ cups

Maple Frosting

4 teaspoons water

1 cup maple sugar

Mix the ingredients together. Let stand for 20 minutes, then spread on cake.

Makes 1 cup

Oatmeal Pie Shell

$^3/_4$ cup oat flour

$^1/_3$ cup hot water

Preheat the oven to 325°F.

Mix the flour and hot water together. Press into a 9-inch pie pan. Prick with a fork all over. Bake for 15 minutes (microwave 3 to 4 minutes) or until done.

Makes 1 pie shell

Old-Fashioned Chocolate Pie

1 cup sugar or honey

$1/3$ cup baking cocoa

$1/4$ cup all-purpose flour

Pinch of salt

$2^1/4$ cups water

1 tablespoon butter or margarine

1 teaspoon vanilla

1 (9-inch) pastry shell, baked
   (such as Oatmeal Pie Shell, see opposite page)

Whipped Cream (see page 306) and chocolate
   sprinkles for garnish (optional)

In a large saucepan, combine the sugar, cocoa, flour, and salt; gradually add the water. Cook and stir over medium heat until the mixture comes to a boil. Cook and stir for 1 minute or until thickened. Remove from the heat and stir in the butter and vanilla. Pour into pastry shell. Refrigerate for 2 to 3 hours before slicing. Garnish with whipped cream and chocolate sprinkles.

Makes 6 to 8 servings

Peach Pie with Almond Crust

1 $1/2$ to 2 cups finely ground unblanched almonds

1 envelope unflavored gelatin

$1/4$ cup hot water

$1/4$ cup cold water

$1/2$ cup honey or sugar

$1/4$ teaspoon sea salt

2 tablespoons pineapple juice or lemon juice

1 $1/2$ cups crushed peaches with juice

Line a 9-inch pie pan with the ground almonds. Combine the gelatin and hot water. Let stand for 3 minutes. Add the cold water and stir until the gelatin is dissolved. Add the honey, salt, and juice. Chill. When partially set, beat until light and fluffy. Fold in the peaches with juice. Gently pour into the prepared shell. Chill until firm (2 to 3 hours).

Makes about 8 servings

Pumpkin Pecan Pie

1 (9-inch) oatmeal pie shell, *unbaked* (recipe, page 286)

3 eggs or egg replacer

1 cup mashed pumpkin

1 to 1³/₄ cups maple sugar, maple syrup, or sugar

1 teaspoon vanilla

1 teaspoon nutmeg (optional)

¹/₄ teaspoon sea salt

1 cup chopped pecans

Preheat the oven to 350°F.

  Mix the eggs with the remaining ingredients and pour into the pie shell. Bake for about 40 minutes.

Makes 6 servings

Rice or Rye Pie Crust

Since this crust is tender, it should be baked in six individual tart pans to eliminate cutting and transferring to a serving plate.

1 cup rice or rye flour

$1/2$ teaspoon sea salt

$1/3$ cup butter or shortening

3 tablespoons cold water

Preheat the oven to 450°F.

Mix the flour and salt. Using a pastry blender or fork, cut in the butter or shortening until the size of peas. Sprinkle with water, a tablespoon at a time. Blend lightly with a fork until all the flour is moistened. Form into a ball. Divide the ball of dough into sixths and roll each section between squares of waxed paper until about $1/8$ inch thick. Remove the top paper. Turn the pastry into 4-inch tart shells. Remove the remaining paper. Carefully fit the pastry into the tart shell. Flute the edges and prick the pastry several times on the bottom and sides with a fork. Repeat for the remaining balls of dough. Bake for 10 to 12 minutes.

Makes 6 tart shells

Strawberry Pie

1 baked oatmeal pie shell (see page 286)

1 envelope unflavored gelatin

$1/4$ cup cold water

$1/2$ cup honey or sugar

$1/4$ teaspoon sea salt

2 tablespoons pineapple juice or lemon juice

$3/4$ cup strawberries, pureed

$3/4$ cup strawberries, sliced

Place the pie shell in a 9-inch pie pan. Combine the gelatin and water. Soak for 3 minutes. Add the honey, salt, juice, and pureed strawberries. Chill. When partially set, fold in the sliced strawberries. Turn into the pie shell. Chill until firm (2 to 3 hours).

Makes 6 servings

Apple Tapioca

$^1/_4$ cup Minute Tapioca

2 $^1/_2$ cups apple juice

Dash of sea salt

$^1/_3$ cup honey or sugar

Mix together all the ingredients and let stand for 5 minutes. Bring to a boil over a medium heat, stirring often. Cool for 20 minutes. Stir well. Serve warm or cold.

Makes 3 to 4 servings

Apple Tapioca Supreme

$^1/_3$ cup Minute Tapioca

$^3/_4$ cup honey or sugar

2 to 3 tart apples, peeled and sliced (about 4 cups)

2 cups water

2 tablespoons pineapple, apple, or lemon juice

2 tablespoons butter or margarine

$^1/_2$ teaspoon sea salt

$^1/_2$ teaspoon nutmeg (optional)

Mix together all the ingredients except the nutmeg in a saucepan and let stand for 5 minutes. Bring to a boil, stirring often. Simmer until the apples are tender (about 12 minutes). Serve with a sprinkle of nutmeg, if desired.

Makes 8 servings

Fruity Rice Pudding

1$\frac{1}{2}$ teaspoons unflavored gelatin

$\frac{1}{4}$ cup cold water

$\frac{1}{3}$ cup hot pineapple juice (or other canned fruit)

2 tablespoons maple sugar, honey, or sugar

$\frac{1}{8}$ teaspoon sea salt

$\frac{1}{2}$ cup rice, cooked

$\frac{1}{2}$ cup diced canned pineapple and/or peaches, drained

1 teaspoon vanilla

Soak the gelatin in cold water. Dissolve the soaked gelatin in the hot pineapple juice. Add the maple sugar and salt. Chill until slightly thickened. Add the cooked rice, fruit, and vanilla. Turn into a mold and chill until firm.

> **Note:** Other fruit combinations can be used.

Makes 4 servings

Hasty Pudding

$^3/_4$ cup maple syrup

$^1/_3$ cup water

$^3/_4$ cup tapioca starch

1 $^1/_2$ teaspoons baking powder

$^1/_2$ teaspoon sea salt

$^1/_4$ cup maple sugar

$^1/_2$ cup nut or goat's milk

1 teaspoon vanilla

$^1/_4$ cup butter or margarine, melted, or oil

$^1/_4$ cup raisins or chopped nuts (optional)

Preheat the oven to 350°F. Grease a 1-quart casserole.

Bring the syrup and water to a boil in a saucepan. Mix the tapioca starch, baking powder, salt, sugar, nut milk, vanilla, and butter in a bowl until smooth. Pour into the casserole dish. Sprinkle with raisins or nuts. Pour the boiling syrup over the batter (it makes a sauce in the bottom of the pan after the pudding is baked). Bake for 35 to 40 minutes. Serve with nut milk, if desired.

Makes 3 to 4 servings

> **VARIATIONS, IF TOLERATED:**
> - Serve warm with light cream.
> - Substitute an equal amount of milk for the nut or goat's milk.
> - Use 1 cup wheat flour in place of the tapioca starch.

Vanilla Pudding

$^1/_4$ cup cornstarch

$^1/_3$ cup sugar

$^1/_8$ teaspoon sea salt

$2^3/_4$ cups milk or water

2 tablespoons butter or margarine

1 teaspoon vanilla

Mix dry ingredients in saucepan. Stir milk in slowly, keeping mixture smooth. Cook over medium heat, stirring continuously, until it comes to a boil. Boil gently 1 minute and take off heat. Stir butter and vanilla into hot pudding. Pour into dishes. Cool and chill.

Makes 8 ($^1/_2$ cup) servings

VARIATIONS, IF TOLERATED:
- For Chocolate Pudding, add 3 tablespoons cocoa. Increase sugar to $^2/_3$ cup. Mix in with cornstarch.

Rice Brown Betty

8 tart apples, peeled, cored, and sliced

$1/2$ cup raisins

$1/2$ cup honey or sugar

$1/2$ cup apple juice or water

$1/4$ cup maple sugar

3 tablespoons rice flour

1 teaspoon nutmeg (optional)

$1/2$ cup rolled oats

$1/2$ cup rice flour

$1/4$ cup honey or sugar

$1/2$ cup sunflower seeds

$1/4$ cup butter or margarine

Preheat the oven to 350°F. Grease an 11 x 17-inch pan.

Combine the apples, raisins, honey, juice, maple sugar, flour, and nutmeg. Turn into the baking pan. Combine the oats, rice flour, honey, sunflower seeds, and butter. Mix well. Spread over the apple mixture. Bake for 45 to 50 minutes.

Makes 9 to 10 servings

VARIATIONS, IF TOLERATED:
- Substitute an equal amount of milk for the apple juice or water.
- Substitute an equal amount of wheat flour for the rice flour.

Rice Pudding

$^{1}/_{4}$ to $^{1}/_{2}$ cup rice, cooked

1 cup nut or goat's milk

$^{1}/_{4}$ cup honey or sugar

1 teaspoon vanilla

$^{1}/_{2}$ cup raisins

Preheat the oven to 325°F. Grease a 9 x 5-inch loaf pan. Mix all the ingredients together and pour into the loaf pan. Bake for about 1 hour.

Makes 6 servings

VARIATIONS, IF TOLERATED:
- Substitute an equal amount of milk for the nut milk.

17.

Staples, Condiments, Sauces, and Spreads

During the elimination or avoidance diet, it can be difficult to find staples that avoid all of the suspected food allergens. In this chapter there are recipes that take the place of such convenience foods as mayonnaise, sour cream, whipped cream, and cottage cheese. There are also recipes for spreads and homemade sauces, including catsup, tomato sauce, white sauce, and tartar sauce.

STAPLES

CORN-FREE BAKING POWDER ... 301

HOMEMADE COTTAGE CHEESE ... 302

OAT NOODLES ... 303

CONDIMENTS

CATSUP ... 304

EGGLESS MAYONNAISE ... 305

WHIPPED CREAM ... 306

SAUCES

QUICK TOMATO SAUCE ... 307

TARTAR SAUCE ... 308

WHITE SAUCE ... 309

SPREADS

APPLE HONEY BUTTER ... 310

BLUEBERRY JAM ... 311

MAPLE BUTTER SPREAD ... 312

NUT BUTTER ... 313

STRAWBERRY JAM ... 314

Corn-Free Baking Powder

$1/4$ cup baking soda

$1/2$ cup cream of tartar

$1/4$ cup potato starch

Sift each ingredient before measuring. Mix together thoroughly and sift again. Keep the baking powder dry in a tightly covered jar. To check if the baking powder is still active, add several drops of water to a small amount. If it bubbles vigorously, the baking powder is still good. Use as you would any commercial double-acting baking powder.

Makes 1 cup

Homemade Cottage Cheese

Any type of milk can be used. Goat's milk works well, either fresh or powdered (combine 7 rounded tablespoons powdered milk with 2^1/$_2$ cups water). This is a fun recipe for kids to help with, since most children have never seen how "curds and whey" are made.

2^1/$_2$ cups milk
1 ^{1}/$_2$ teaspoons rennet
Sea salt to taste (optional)

In a saucepan, heat the milk until just tepid. Add the rennet and mix well. Pour the milk into a bowl and leave it in a warm place for 15 minutes, or until the milk has set and curds have formed. Pour the milk mixture into the top of a double boiler and gently heat over hot water to a temperature of 110°F (slightly warmer than lukewarm). Stir constantly until the curds and whey separate. Put a strainer over a bowl and line it with several layers of cheesecloth. Pour in the curds and whey. Tie the corners of the cheesecloth together to form a bag and suspend the bag over the bowl for 12 to 24 hours to drain. The cheese can be drained in 2 to 3 hours by gently squeezing the bag from time to time. Put the drained curds in a bowl, mash it with a fork, and season it to taste. For extra flavor, herbs or spices can be added. Covered and stored in the refrigerator, the cottage cheese will keep for up to one week.

Makes 4 ounces

Oat Noodles

These noodles can be dried and then stored in an airtight container. They can also be frozen for later use.

1 cup oat flour

$^1/_2$ teaspoon sea salt

$^1/_4$ cup water

Sift the flour and salt together in a large bowl. Form a well in the center of the flour mixture and add the water. Slowly stir the flour into the water until combined. Cover the bowl and let stand for an hour.

On an oat-floured board, roll out the dough $^1/_{16}$ inch thick. Cut into strips 1 inch thick, then slice each strip crosswise into $^1/_4$ to $^1/_2$-inch-wide noodles. Spread the noodles out on a floured surface and allow to dry for several hours. Cook in plenty of boiling, salted water for 10 to 12 minutes.

Makes 4 servings

VARIATIONS, IF TOLERATED:
- Beat one egg into the water until frothy.
- Substitute other types of flour for the oat flour.

Catsup

$^1/_2$ cup apple cider vinegar

$^1/_2$ teaspoon cloves

1 teaspoon nutmeg

$^1/_2$ teaspoon celery seed

4 pounds tomatoes (about 12 medium tomatoes),
   washed and quartered, stem removed

$^1/_4$ cup water

$^1/_4$ cup honey or sugar

2 teaspoons sea salt

Combine the vinegar, cloves, nutmeg, and celery seed in a small covered saucepan. Bring to a boil. Remove from the heat and let stand. In a large kettle or Dutch oven, cook the tomatoes and water over medium heat until the tomatoes are quite soft. Put the tomato mixture through a sieve or food mill and return to the heat. Add the honey or sugar and salt. Bring to a boil. Reduce the heat and simmer until the volume has been reduced by half. Strain the vinegar mixture into the tomato mixture. Continue simmering until the desired consistency is reached, stirring frequently. Cool and refrigerate in a covered container.

Makes 2 cups

Eggless Mayonnaise

1$\frac{1}{2}$ tablespoons rice flour

$\frac{1}{2}$ teaspoon sea salt

$\frac{1}{4}$ teaspoon dry mustard

$\frac{1}{4}$ cup cold water

$\frac{3}{4}$ cup boiling water

1 tablespoon apple cider vinegar

$\frac{1}{2}$ cup safflower oil

Additional sea salt to taste (optional)

In a medium-size pan, combine the flour, salt, dry mustard, and cold water and stir well. Add the boiling water. Stir constantly over medium heat until the mixture thickens and comes to a boil. Cool until lukewarm. Combine the vinegar and oil and add to the mixture slowly, beating constantly. When well blended, mix in additional salt to taste. Refrigerate in a covered container.

Makes 1$\frac{1}{2}$ to 2 cups

Whipped Cream

$^1/_2$ cup nut milk

$^1/_4$ teaspoon vanilla

$^1/_2$ cup safflower oil

1 tablespoon honey

Pinch of sea salt

Put the nut milk and vanilla in a blender and blend at medium speed. With blender running, gradually add the oil until the mixture becomes very thick. If necessary, add a little more oil. Blend in the honey and salt.

Makes 1 cup

Quick Tomato Sauce

I use this recipe all the time when I make spaghetti sauce.

1 (6-ounce) can pure tomato paste

1 $\frac{1}{2}$ cups water

1 tablespoon fresh basil, minced, or other seasonings

1 teaspoon honey or sugar

In a medium-size saucepan, add the ingredients and simmer for 5 minutes.

Makes 2 cups

Tartar Sauce

1 cup eggless mayonnaise (see page 305)

2 tablespoons sweet pickles, if allowed, chopped

1 teaspoon dried parsley, minced

$^1/_4$ teaspoon dry mustard

Mix all ingredients thoroughly and chill. Serve over fish.

Makes 1 cup

White Sauce

Butter, of course, is preferred, but you can use beef fat or vegetable oil. You are making a roux (roo), a classic French sauce made from a paste of butter and flour with milk slowly stirred in. Since you probably can't have this mixture, keep notes of your ingredients until you get a sauce that pleases you.

1 tablespoon butter

$1^{1}/_{2}$ teaspoons potato starch

$^{1}/_{4}$ teaspoon sea salt

$^{1}/_{2}$ cup allowed milk

1 teaspoon dried parsley (optional)

Melt the butter in a saucepan over medium heat. Add the potato starch or flour and salt and stir until mixed well. Add the milk and parsley. Continue to stir until the mixture thickens.

Makes $^{3}/_{4}$ cups

> **VARIATIONS, IF TOLERATED:**
> - In place of potato starch, try Cream of Rice, or Minute Tapioca. Also try wheat, rice, or barley flour and increase or decrease the amount of liquid to thicken the sauce.

Apple Honey Butter

You could can the apple butter, but I just put it in glass or plastic jars and freeze them. I used to live in Goshen, Indiana, near many Amish farmers. In the fall, they would make the best apple butter and sell it in many quaint stores all around the area. My favorite restaurant and bakery was Amish Acres in Nappanee. Every week we would go for their world-famous meals and, of course, to buy out half the bakery.

$3^1/2$ pounds apples, peeled, cored, and chopped
1 to $1^1/2$ cups honey
$^1/2$ cup apple cider vinegar
$^1/2$ cup crushed pineapple

Preheat the oven to 300°F.

In a medium-size saucepan over low heat, cook the apples until soft. (No water is necessary, since there is enough moisture in the apples.) Puree in a blender to make 8 cups of applesauce. Combine the applesauce with honey, vinegar, and pineapple in a large 6-quart pan. Bake for 3 hours, stirring often. Pour hot into pint jars; cool and refrigerate.

Makes 6 cups

Blueberry Jam

You can make extra jars of strawberry or blueberry jam and give them away as gifts. It doesn't matter what time of year since frozen berries work as well as fresh ones!

4 cups fresh blueberries or other berry

2 cups sugar

1 envelope unflavored gelatin

1 teaspoon lemon extract

In a large saucepan, slightly crush half the berries. Add the remaining berries, sugar, and gelatin. Heat to boiling, stirring constantly. Boil hard for 2 minutes, stirring constantly. Stir in the lemon extract. Pour into clean jelly glasses or jars. Seal the jars or freeze.

Makes 3 half-pints

Maple Butter Spread

This is so rich and delicious when you spread this warm, gooey, thick sauce over homemade biscuits, scones, or pancakes. It's perfect for weekend brunches when everyone can sit and relax at the table, enjoying these homemade treats.

1 cup maple syrup
$^3/_4$ cup butter, melted

Cook the maple syrup over medium heat until a small amount forms a soft ball in cold water. Add the butter and beat until thick and creamy. Serve warm on waffles or hot biscuits and cold on slices of bread. Keep refrigerated.

Makes 1$^1/_2$ cups

Nut Butter

You can use any nut you want. Cashews are the creamiest. Try cashew nut oil or almond nut oil. Remember to refrigerate the delicate nut oils as they go rancid very quickly.

1$^1/_2$ cups chopped almonds or cashews
1 to 3 tablespoons safflower or nut oil
$^1/_4$ teaspoon sea salt

Preheat the oven to 350°F.

Spread the nuts in a shallow pan. Sprinkle with oil and salt. Bake for 10 to 15 minutes or until toasted. Place the nuts in a blender. Process at medium speed until smooth and creamy. You may have to push the nut mixture down once or twice to get it well-blended. Pour into a covered container. Store in the refrigerator or freezer. Since the nut butter is not homogenized, the oil will rise to the top. Stir to blend in the oil before using.

Makes 1 cup

Strawberry Jam

2 tablespoons lemon juice

1 envelope unflavored gelatin

2 tablespoons water

1$^1/_2$ teaspoons arrowroot or cornstarch

2 cups fresh strawberries

4 to 4$^1/_2$ tablespoons honey, maple syrup, or sugar

Combine the lemon juice, gelatin, water, and arrowroot. Heat in a saucepan, stirring constantly. Lower the heat, add the berries and sweetener, and heat to boiling. Boil for 3 minutes or more until strawberries are the right consistency. Pour into jars and refrigerate or freeze.

> **Note:** You can also use frozen, unsweetened strawberries. Just thaw and drain first.

Makes 2 cups

Appendix

Biological Classification of Foods

The following list contains the name of a common food and the name of its biological food family. Familiarizing yourself with these charts will enable you to check on food families to which you may be sensitive. For example: If you are allergic to tomatoes, you may also be sensitive to eggplant or potatoes. (See potato family listing.) Or, if grains are a problem, you can substitute items from different families such as tapioca starch (spurge family) or potato starch (potato family). By being aware of these food families, you can avoid items to which you may be cross-sensitive and find appropriate substitutes.

Food	Family	Food	Family
A		Boysenberry	Rose
Acacia gum	Carob	Bran (wheat)	Grain
Alfafa	Legume	Brazil nut	Lecythis
Allspice	Myrtle	Breadfruit	Mulberry
Almond	Plum	Broccoli	Mustard
Amaranth	Amaranth	Brussels Sprouts	Mustard
Anise	Parsley	Buckwheat	Buckwheat
Apple	Apple	Butternut (White walnut)	Walnut
Apricot	Plum		
Arrowroot	Arrowroot	**C**	
Artichoke, Common	Composite	Cabbage: celery cabbage, common	Mustard
Artichoke, Jerusalem	Composite		
Asparagus	Lily	Caffeine	Madder, Stercula
Avocado	Laurel		
		Cane	Grain
B		Cantaloupe	Gourd
Bamboo shoots	Grain	Capers	Capers
Banana	Banana	Caraway	Parsley
Barley	Grain	Cardamom	Ginger
Basil	Mint	Carob	Carob
Bay leaf	Laurel	Carrageen	Red Algae
Bean: kidney, lima, mung, navy	Legume	Carrot	Parsley
		Casaba	Gourd
Beet: common, sugar	Goosefoot	Cashew	Cashew
		Cassava	Spurge
Blackberry	Rose		
Blueberry	Heath		

Food	Family	Food	Family
Cauliflower	Mustard	Comfrey	Borage
Celeriac	Parsley	Coriander	Parsley
Celery	Parsley	Corn	Grain
Celtuce	Composite	Cotton, Cottonseed	Mallow
Chamomile	Composite	Coumarin	Legume
Chard, Swiss	Goosefoot	Cranberry	Heath
Cherimoya	Pawpaw	Cream of Tartar	Grape
Chervil	Parsley	Cucumber	Gourd
Cherry	Plum	Cumin	Parsley
Chestnut	Beach	Currant	Gooseberry
Chestnut Chinese	Water Chestnut	**D**	
Chestnut, horse	Oak	Dandelion	Composite
Chicle	Sapodillo	Dasheen	Arum
Chicory	Composite	Date	Palm
Chive	Lily	Dewberry	Rose
Chocolate	Stercula	Dextrose	Grain
Christmas melon	Gourd	Dill	Parsley
Cider	Apple, Grain	Dulse	Red Algae
Cinnamon	Laurel		
Citron	Citrus	**E**	
Citronella	Grain	Eggplant	Potato
Clove	Myrtle	Elderberry	Honeysuckle
Clover	Legume	Endive	Composite
Cocoa	Stercula	Escarole	Composite
Coconut	Palm		
Coffee	Madder	**F**	
Cola (Kola)	Stercula	Fennel	Parsley
Collard	Mustard	Fenugreek	Legume
Colza shoots	Mustard	Fig	Mulberry

Food	Family	Food	Family
Filbert	Birch	Juniper	Pine

G

		K	
Garlic	Lily	Kale	Mustard
Gherkin	Gourd	Karaya gum	Stercula
Ginger	Ginger	Kowi	Actinidia
Ginseng	Ginseng	Kohlrabi	Mustard
Goldenrod	Composite	Kumquat	Citrus
Gooseberry	Gooseberry		
Graham (Wheat)	Grain	**L**	
Grape	Grape	Lamb's quarters	Goosefoot
Grapefruit	Citrus	Lavender	Mint
Ground cherry	Potato	Leek	Lily
Guaiacgum	Caltrap	Lemon	Citrus
Gava	Myrtle	Lentil	Legume
		Lettuce	Composite
H		Licorice	Legume
Hazelnut	Birch	Lime	Citrus
Hickory	Walnut	Linseed (Flax)	Flax
Honey	Miscellan- eous	Litchi Nut	Soapberry
		Loganberry	Rose
Honeydew	Gourd	Lovage	Parsley
Hops	Mulberry		
Horehound	Mint	**M**	
Horseradish	Mustard	Macadamia nut	Macadamia
Huckleberry	Heath	Mace	Nutmeg
		Malanga	Arum
J		Malt, Maltose	Grain
Jicama	Morning Glory	Mango	Cashew
		Maple, Maple Sugar	Maple

Food	Family	Food	Family
Marjoram	Mint	Paprika	Myrtle
Mate	Holly	Parsley	Parsley
May Apple	May Apple	Parsnip	Parsley
Melon: Musk, Persian	Gourd	Pawpaw	Pawpaw
Millet	Grain	Peach	Plum
Mint	Mint	Peanut	Legume
Molasses (treacle)	Goosefoot, Grain	Pear	Apple
		Pear, prickly	Cactus
Mulberry	Mulberry	Peas: black-eye, chick-pea	Legume
Mushroom	Fungi		
Muskmelon	Gourd	Pecan	Walnut
Mustard	Mustard	Pectin	Apple
		Pepper	Pepper
N		Pepper, garden	Potato
Nectarine	Plum	Peppermint	Mint
New Zealand Spinach	Purslane	Persimmon	Ebony
Nutmeg	Nutmeg	Pimento	Myrtle
		Pimiento	Potato
O		Pineapple	Pineapple
Oats	Grain	Pine nut	Pine
Okra	Mallow	Pistachio	Cashew
Olive	Olive	Plantain	Banana
Onion	Lily	Plum	Plum
Orange	Citrus	Poi	Arum
Oregano	Mint	Pomegranate	Pomegranate
Oyster plant	Composite	Poppy seed	Poppy
		Potato	Potato
P		Potato, Chinese	Yam
Palm cabbage	Palm	Potato, sweet	Morning Glory
Papain	Papal		
Papaya	Papal		

Food	Family
Pumpkin	Gourd
Purslane	Purslane
Pyrethrum	Composite

Q

Food	Family
Quince	Apple

R

Food	Family
Radish	Mustard
Ragweed	Composite
Raisin	Grape
Raspberry	Rose
Rhubarb	Buckwheat
Rice	Grain
Rose Hips	Rose
Rosemary	Mint
Rutabaga	Mustard
Rye	Grain

S

Food	Family
Safflower	Composite
Saffron	Iris
Sage	Mint
Sagebrush	Composite
Sago	Palm
Salsify	Composite
Sapota	Sapodilla
Sarsparilla	Lily

Food	Family
Sassafras	Laurel
Savory	Mint
Senna	Legume
Sepote	Sepote
Sesame	Pedalium
Sorghum	Grain
Sorrel	Buckwheat
Soybean	Legume
Spearmint	Mint
Spinach	Goosefoot
Spinach, New Zealand	Purslane
Squash	Gourd
Starfruit	Carambola
Strawberry	Rose
Sugar, beet	Goosefoot
Sugar, cane	Grain
Sugar, corn	Grain
Sugar, maple	Maple
Sunflower	Composite
Sweet Potato	Morning Glory

T

Food	Family
Tangerine	Citrus
Tapioca	Spurge
Taro	Arum
Tarragon	Composite
Tea	Tea
Tequilla	Cactuato Morning Glory

Food	Family	Food	Family
Thistle	Goosefoot	Youngberry	Rose
Thyme	Mint	Yuca	Spurge
Tobacco	Potato	Yucca	Lilly
Tomato	Potato		
Tragacanth gum	Legume	**Z**	
Tritical	Grain	Zucchini	Gourd
Turmeric	Ginger		
Turnip	Mustard		

V

Food	Family
Vanilla	Orchid
Vinegar	Apple, Grains, Grape

W

Food	Family
Walnut	Walnut
Water celery	Parsley
Water chestnuts, Chinese	Chinese Water Chestnut
Watercress	Mustard
Watermelon	Gourd
Wheat	Grain
Wintergreen	Heath
Wintergreen (Oil of Birch)	Birch

Y

Food	Family
Yam	Yam
Yautia	Arum
Yeast	Fungi

BIOLOGICAL FOOD FAMILIES

Here you can check the different biological food families and familiarize yourself with what foods belong to each family.

VEGETABLE CLASSIFICATIONS

Apple Family
Apple
  Cider
  Juice
  Vinegar
  Apple pectin
Pear
Quince
  Quince seed

Arrowroot Family
Arrowroot

Arum Family
Dasheen
Malanga
Taro
  Poi
Yautia

Banana Family
Banana
Plantain

Beech Family
Beechnut
Chestnut

Birch Family
Filbert
Hazelnut
Oil of birch
(wintergreen)

Borage Family
Borage
Comfrey

Brazilnut Family
Brazil nut

Buckwheat Family
Buckwheat
Rhubarb
Sorrel

Cactus Family
Prickly pear
Tequila

Caltrap Family
Gum guaiac

Caper Family
Capers

Cashew Family
Cashew
Mango
Pistachio

Chinese Water Chestnut Family
Chestnuts, Chinese

Citrus Family
Citron
Grapefruit
Kumquat
Lemon
Lime
Orange
Tangerine

Composite Family
Absinthe
Artichoke, Common
Celtuce
Chamomile
Chicory
Dandelion
Endive
Escarole

Goldenrod
Lettuce
  Head
  Leaf
Jerusalem artichoke
Oyster plant
  Salsify
Ragweed and
  Pyrethrum and other
  related inhalants
Romaine lettuce
Safflower
Sesame seed
Sunflower
Sagebrush
  Wormwood
Tarragon

Ebony Family
Persimmon

Fungi Family
Mushroom
Yeast

Ginger Family
Cardamom
Ginger
Turmeric

Ginseng Family
Ginseng

Gooseberry Family
Currant
Gooseberry

Goosefoot Family
Beet
  Beet sugar
Chard
  Swiss chard
Lamb's quarters
Spinach
Thistle

Gourd Family
Cantaloupe
Casaba
Christmas melon
Cucumber
Gherkin
Honeydew
Muskmelon
Persian melon
Pumpkin
Squash
  Summer
  Winter
Watermelon
Zucchini

Grain (Cereal, Grasses) Family
Barley
  Malt
  Maltose
Bamboo shoots
Cane
  Cane sugar
  Turbinado

Rum
Corn
Cornmeal
Cornstarch
Corn oil
Corn sugar
Dextrose
Corn syrup
Glucose
Grits
Hominy
  Whiskey/bourbon
Millet
Oats
Popcorn
Rice
Rye
Sorghum
  Kafir
  Molasses
Triticale
Wheat
  Bran
  "Farina"
Flour
  Graham
  Gluten
  Semolina flour
Wheat germ
Wild rice

Grape Family
Grape
  Brandy (grape)
  Champagne

Cream of tartar
Raisin
Grape wine
Vinegar

Heath Family
Blueberry
Cranberry
Huckleberry
Wintergreen

Holly Family
Bearberry
Maté (or yerba maté)
Pokeberry
Yaupon tea

Honeysuckle Family
Elderberry

Iris Family
Saffron

Kelp Family
Algin

Laurel Family
Avocado
Bay Leaf
Cinnamon
Sassafras

Legume Family
Alfalfa
Black-eyed pea
Bush bean
Carob

Chick-pea
  (garbanzo)
Green bean
Green pea
Jack bean
Kidney bean
Lentil
Licorice
Lima bean
Mung bean
Navy bean
Pea
Peanut
  Peanut oil
Pinto bean
Senna
Soybean
  Soybean Flour
  Soybean Oil
  Lecithin
String bean
Tonka bean
Tragacanth gum

Lily Family
Aloe
Asparagus
Bermuda onion
Chive
Garlic
Leek
Onion
Sarsaparilla
Yucca

Macadamia Family
Macadamia nut

Madder Family
Coffee

Mallow Family
Cottonseed
  Cottonseed Meal
  Cottonseed Oil
Okra (gumbo)

Maple Family
Maple sugar
Maple syrup

May Apple Family
May apple

Mint Family
Artichoke, Chinese
Basil
Horehound
Lavender
Marjoram
Mint
Oregano
Peppermint
Rosemary
Sage
Savory
Spearmint
Thyme

Morning Glory Family
Sweet potato

Mulberry Family
Breadfruit
Fig
Hops
Mulberry

Mustard Family
Broccoli
Brussels sprout
Cabbage
Cauliflower
Celery cabbage
Collard
Colza shoot
Horseradish
Kale
Kohlrabi
Mustard
Radish
Rutabaga
Turnip
Watercress

Myrtle Family
Allspice
Cloves
Guava
Paprika
Peppermint
Pimento
Rosemary

Nutmeg Family
Mace
Nutmeg

Oak Family
Chestnut

Olive Family
Black olive (ripe)
  Olive oil
Green olive

Orchid Family
Vanilla

Palm Family
Coconut
  Coconut Oil
Date
Palm cabbage
Sago

Papal Family
Papaya
  Papain

Parsley Family
Angelica
Anise
Caraway
Carrot
Celeriac
Celery
Celery seed
Chervil
Coriander
Cumin
Dill
Fennel
Lovage
Parsley
Parsnip
Water celery

Pawpaw Family
Pawpaw

Pepper Family
Black pepper
White pepper

Pine Family
Juniper
Piñon nut (pignolia)
  Pine nut

Pineapple Family
Pineapple

Plum Family
Almond
Apricot
Cherry
  Sour Cherry
  Sweet Cherry
Nectarine
Peach
Plum
  Prune

Pomegranate Family
Pomegranate

Poppy Family
Poppy seed

Potato (Nightshade) Family
Belladonna
Eggplant
Ground cherry
Peppers
  Chili
  Cayenne
  Red
  Green
  Red sweet
  Paprika
Potato
Tobacco
Tomato

Purslane Family
New Zealand spinach
Purslane

Rose Family
Blackberry
Boysenberry
Dewberry
Loganberry
Raspberry
  Black
  Red
Strawberry
Youngberry

Sapodilla Family
Chicle

Soapberry Family
Litchi nut

Spurge Family
Cassava (Yuca)
Tapioca

Sterculia Family
Cacao
  Chocolate
  Cocoa

Cola
Karava gum
Kola bean

Tea Family
Tea
  Black
  Green

Walnut Family
Butternut
Hickory
Pecan
Walnut
  Black
  English

Yam Family
Chinese potato
Yam

Miscellaneous
Honey

ANIMAL CLASSIFICATIONS

Amphibian Family
Frog

Bird Family
Chicken
  Chicken eggs
Duck
  Duck eggs
Goose
  Goose eggs
Grouse
Guinea hen
Partridge
Peacock
Pheasant
Pigeon
Quail
Squab
Turkey

Crustacean Family
Decapods
  Crab
  Crayfish
  Lobster
  Prawn
  Shrimp

Mammal Family
Antelope
Bear
Beaver
  Bovine
  Beef (cattle)
  Butter
  Cheese
  Gelatin (beef)
  Lactose (milk sugar)
  Cow's milk
  Veal
Bison
Buffalo
Goat
  Goat Milk
  Goat Cheese
Sheep
  Lamb
  Mutton
Deer
  Caribou
  Deer (venison)
  Elk
  Moose
  Reindeer
Dolphin
Pig (pork)
  Bacon
  Ham
  Lard
Rabbit
  Cottontail
  Hare
  Jackrabbit
Squirrel
Whale

Mollusk Family
Cephalopods
  Octopus
  Squid
Gastropods
  Abalone
  Snail (escargot)
Pelecypods
  Clam
  Cockle
  Mussel
  Oyster
  Quahog
  Scallop

Reptile Family
Alligator
Rattlesnake
Turtle

Fish (Saltwater)

Anchovy Family
Anchovy

Barracuda Family
Barracuda

Bluefish Family
Bluefish

Codfish Family
Cod (scrod)
Cusk
Haddock

Hake
Pollack

Croaker Family
Croaker
Drum
Sea trout
Silver perch
Spot
Weakfish
  (spotted sea trout)

Dolphin Family
Dolphin

Eel Family
American eel

Flounder Family
Dab

Flounder
Halibut
Plaice
Sole
Turbot

**Harvest Fish
Family**
Butterfish
Harvest fish

Herring Family
Menhaden
Pilchard (sardine)
Sea herring
Shad

Jack Family
Aberjack
Pompano
Yellow jack

Mackerel Family
Albacore
Bonito
Mackerel
Skipjack
Tuna

Marlin Family
Marlin
Sailfish

Mullet Family
Mullet

Porgy Family
Northern scup (porgy)

Sea Bass Family
Grouper
Sea bass
Red snapper

**Scorpion Fish
Family**
Rosefish
  (ocean perch)

**Sea Catfish
Family**
Ocean catfish

Shark Family
Shark
Monk

Silverside Family
Silverside (whitebait)

Swordfish Family
Swordfish

Tarpon Family
Tarpon
Tilefish Family
  Tilefish

Fish (Freshwater)

Bass Family
White perch
Yellow bass

Catfish Family
Bullhead
Catfish species

Croaker Family
Freshwater drum

Herring Family
Shad (roe)

Minnow Family
Carp
Chub

Paddlefish Family
Paddlefish

Perch Family
Sauger
Walleye, Pike
Yellow perch

Pike Family
Pickerel
Pike, Northern
Muskellunge

Salmon Family
Salmon species
Trout species

Smelt Family
Smelt

Sturgeon Family
Sturgeon (caviar)

Sucker Family
Buffalofish
Sucker

Sunfish Family
Black bass species
Sunfish species
Crappie

Whitefish Family
Whitefish

Index

A

Allergies, food: delayed reactions, 23, 24; diagnosis of, 15, 18; identifying allergens, 37–54; immediate reactions, 22–23; inhalation of odors and, 20; notebook on, organization of, 25–26; outgrowing, 23; permanent, 23; symptoms of, 15, 22, 23–24; symptoms of, record of, 25, 26; testing for, 17

Allowed foods, 56–71

Almond(s): Biscuits, 141; Bread, Apricot, 127; Butter, 313; Cookies, 244; Crescents, 245; Fish Amandine, 232; Green Beans with, 215; Peach Pie with Almond Crust, 288; Salad, Mandarin, 170

Almond nut milk, 69

Amaranth, 75–76; Granola, 149

Anaphylactic shock, 23, 50, 53

Antihistamines, 18

Apple(s), 62; Butter, Honey, 310; Cooler, Fresh, 117; Crisp, 258; freezing, 101; Granola, Nutmeg, 147, 150; Maple Sweet Potato Bake, 217; Oatmeal, 151; Oatmeal, Spice, 152; pudding, tapioca, 292, 293; Rice Betty, 259; Rice Brown Betty, 297; Salad, Gelatin, 161; Salad, Sunny Fruit, 177; Scalloped, 266; Snack, 268

Apple juice, 62; Dressing, Honey, 184; Tapioca, 292

Applesauce, 62, 260; Cookies, 246; Shake, Apricot-Apple, 113

Apricot(s): Bread, Almond, 127; Granola, Amaranth, 149; Shake, -Apple, 113

Arrowroot, 62–63

Avocado(s): Salad, Almond Orange, 162–63; Tuna Stuffed, 163

Avoidance diet, 15, 16–19; cravings, 20–21; maintenance diet, 22; physician's guidelines, 16; setbacks and deviation from, 19–20; testing foods, 21–22

B

Baking powder, 63–64; Biscuits, 35; Corn-Free, 63–64, 301

Baking products, 56

Banana(s), 64; Bread, 128; Cake, 275; Cookies, Oatmeal, 247; Cooler, -Pineapple, 113; Crisp, Oatmeal, 271; Date Yam Supreme, 212; Drink, -Peach, 114; freezing, 64, 101, 115; French-Fried, 261; Frosty Freezer Treats, 101, 262; Jamaican Baked, 264; Kabobs, Orange Vegetable, 220–21; Muffins, Oat, 139; Muffins, Rice Flour, 140; Salad, Honey, 164; Salad, Sunflower, 176; Shake, 115; Shake, Tropical, 123

Bar cookies: Brownies, 250; Chocolate Crunch Nut Butter, 252; Nut Butter Granola, 255

Barley, 74; Pilaf, Mushroom and, 206

Barley flour: Bread, Banana, 128; Bread, Zucchini Nut, 136; Cake, Butterscotch Chiffon Tube, 276; Cookies, Barley Drop, 248; Cookies, Honey Nut Raisin, 253; Muffins, Blueberry Oat, 136

Bean(s): Minestrone, 198; Soup, Navy Bean, 199

Beef, 18; Burgers, Broiled, 227; Meat Loaf, Quick Savory, 239; sauce, spaghetti, 100–101; Sloppy Joes, 240; Soup, Vegetable, 202; Stew, Vegetable and, 189; Stock, 190

Beverages, 111; allowed foods, 56; Apple Cooler, Fresh, 117; Apricot-Apple Shake, 113; Banana-Peach Drink, 114; Banana-Pineapple Cooler, 113; Banana Shake, 115; Carrot Milk, 116; Cocoa, Hot, 119; Coconut Milk, 116; Fruit Slush, 118; juices, 68; Kiwifruit Spritzer, 120; Lemonade, 121; Melon Shake, Fresh, 117; Tomato Juice Cocktail, 122; Tropical Shake, 123

Biological classifications of foods, 315–29; alphabetical quick chart, 316–21; animals, 327; fish, 328–29; vegetables, 322–26

Birthday parties, 93–94

Biscuits and scones, 124; Almond, 141; Baking-Powder, 35; Dried Cherry Spelt, 142–43; Oatcakes, Scottish, 144; Rice Flour, 143

Blender breakfast, 147

Blender Broiled Frosting, 283

Blueberry(ies): Cookies, Delight, 249; Jam, 311; Muffins, Oat, 136; Sherbet, 263

Bracelets, Medic-Alert, 23

Breads, quick, 124; Apricot Almond, 127; Banana, 128; Carrot, 129; Coffee Cake, Streusel-Topped, 131; Oatmeal, 130; Rye Crisps, 146; Zucchini Nut, 132

Breads, yeast, 124; Pumpernickel, 133–34; Rice Flour Bread, 134–35

Breakfast dishes, 147; Granola, Amaranth, 149; Granola, Apple Nutmeg, 147, 150; Granola, Crunchy, 153; Oatmeal, Apple, 151; Oatmeal, Apple Spice, 152; Pancake Batter, 155; Pancakes, Dutch Potato, 154; Pancakes, Potato, 156; Waffle Batter, 155; Waffles, Rice, 157

Broth/stock, 64, 190, 193

Brownies, 250

Buckwheat, 65, 74

Butter, 65

Butter(s): Apple Honey, 310; Maple, 312; Nut, 69, 313

Butterscotch Chiffon Tube Cake, 276

Butterscotch Cookies, 251

C

Cabbage: Coleslaw, Overnight, 173; Salad, Sunny Fruit, 177; Soup, Vegetable Beef, 202

Cake(s), 272; Banana, 275; Butterscotch Chiffon Tube, 276; Chiffon "Pound", 277; Chocolate, Quick, 280; Fruity Spice, 278; Oatmeal-Raisin Carrot, 279–80; Rice Spice, 281; Tapioca Pineapple, 282

Candy, Carob, 269

Cantaloupe Sherbet, 261

Carob powder, 65, 84; Candy, 269; Cocoa, Hot, 119

Carrot(s): Bread, 129; Cake, Oatmeal-Raisin, 279–80; Dilled, 213; Maple, 218; Milk, 116; Salad, Sunflower, 176; Salad, Sunny Fruit, 177; Soup, Vegetable Beef, 202; Stew, Beef and Vegetable, 189

Casein, 44, 45–46

Cashew(s): Butter, 313; Salad, Chicken Rice, 166

Casseroles, 99–100; Date Yam Supreme, 212; Maple Apple Sweet Potato Bake, 217; Sweet Potato, Baked, 205

Catsup, 66, 304

Celery, Braised, 207

Celery Seed Salad Dressing, 183

Cellophane noodles, 208

Cheese, 45, 46

Cherry(ies): Duck, Orange and, 228; Scones, Dried Cherry Spelt, 142–43

Chicken: Baked, with Tomato Rice Stuffing, 226; biological classifications, 327; Broth, 193; Chop Suey, 229; Honey Baked, 234; Loaf, 230; Soup, 192; Soup, Potato and, 191; Supreme, 231

Chicken salad(s): Fresh Fruit with, 167; Ginger Mayonnaise, 168; Grape, 165; Hawaiian, 169; Rice, with Cashews, 166; Wild Rice, 180

Chiffon "Pound" Cake, 277

Children and allergies: avoidance diet and cravings, 21; avoidance diet setbacks, 23; eating away from home, 90–92; emergency information form, 87; holidays celebrations, 93–97; lunches at school, 86, 88; lunch suggestions, 88–90, 101; notebook for, 85; outgrowing allergies, 23; overnight stays with friends, 85; peanut allergies and, 53; reactions, types of, 23; reward book, 85; well-balanced diets, 28

China Bowl Rice Sticks, 208

Chocolate: Bars, Nut Butter, 252; Brownies, 250; Cake, Quick, 280; -free cooking, 84; Pie, Old-Fashioned, 287; substitution for, 65

Christmas, 95–96

Cinnamon, 16, 17, 22

Citrus fruit, 16, 17; Dressing, 162–63; See also Lemon(s); Orange(s)

Cocoa, Hot, 119

Coconut, 66; Frosting, Blender Broiled, 283; Icing, Confetti, 284; Raisins,

-Covered, 270; Shake, Tropical, 123

Coconut milk, 66, 69, 116

Coffee, 16, 17

Coffee Cake, Streusel-Topped, 131

Confetti Icing, 284

Confetti Rice, 209

Cookies: Almond, 244; Almond Crescents, 245; Applesauce, 246; Banana Oatmeal, 247; Barley Drop, 248; Blueberry Delight, 249; Butterscotch, 251; Honey Nut Raisin, 253; Pecan Balls, 256; Raisin Nut, 257; See also Bar cookies

Cooking tips, 32, 99–101

Corn, 16, 17; Chowder, 194; -containing foods, 41–43; -Free Baking Powder, 63–64, 301; -free cooking, 79

Cornish Hens, Honey Baked, 235

Cornmeal: Muffins, Corn, 137

Cornstarch: paper goods and, 70; substitution for, 62–63

Cottage Cheese, Homemade, 302

Crackers, 124; Oatmeal, 145; Rye Crisps, 146

Cranberry Relish, 223

Crustaceans, 51; See also Shellfish and seafood

Cucumber Noodles, 211

D

Date sugar, 66, 71, 83

Date Yam Supreme, 212

Dessert(s): Apple Crisp, 258; Apple Rice Betty, 259; Apples, Scalloped, 266; Bananas, French-Fried, 261; Bananas, Jamaican Baked, 264; Crisp, Banana Oatmeal, 271; Frosty Freezer Treats, 101, 262; Pears, Baked, 260; Pineapple Porcupines, 265; Rice Brown Betty, 297; Sherbet, Cantaloupe, 261; Sherbet, Fruit, 263; Sherbet, Watermelon, 267; See also Cake(s); Cookies; Pie(s)

Diary, food, 17, 22, 25–29

Diet: liquid or soft, 96–97; well-balanced, 28; See also Avoidance diet

Dilled Carrots, 213

Duck, Cherry and Orange, 228

E

Easter, 94–95

Egg(s): -containing foods, 44; FALCPA and, 16; -free cooking, 80–81

Eggless Mayonnaise, 305

Eggplant with Tomato, 214

Egg replacer, 67, 80

Elimination diet. See Avoidance diet

Emergency information form, 87

EpiPens, 23

F

Fish: allergies to, 50; allowed foods, 59; Amandine, 232; biological classifications, 328–29; FALCPA and, 16; Flounder Florentine, 233;
Salmon Salad, 175; shopping for, 67; See also Tuna

Flounder Florentine, 233

Flours: allowed foods, 57; substitutions for, 62–63, 65, 67, 73–78; See also specific kinds of flour

Food Allergy Labeling and Consumer Protection Act (FALCPA), 16, 37–39, 48

French Dressing, 158, 184

French-Fried Bananas, 261

Frosting and icing: Blender Broiled, 283; Confetti, 284; Honey Butter, 285; Maple, 285

Frosty Freezer Treats, 101, 262

Fruit(s): allowed foods, 58–59; Cake, Spice, 278; Pudding, Rice, 294; Salad, Molded Gelatin, 171; Salad, Sunny, 177; Sherbet, 263; shopping for, 68; Slush, 118; syrups, 83; See also specific fruits

G

Garlic, 16, 17

Ginger Mayonnaise, 168

Gluten-free baked goods, 73

Goat's milk, 45, 69

Grains, 57

Granola: Amaranth, 149; Apple Nutmeg, 147, 150; Crunchy, 153

Grape(s): Chicken Salad, 165; Chicken Salad with Fresh Fruit, 167

Greek Lemon Soup, 197

Green Beans with Almonds, 215

Grocery shopping, 19, 30–31, 55

H

Halloween, 95
Hash Brown Potatoes, 216
Hasty Pudding, 295
Hawaiian Chicken Salad, 169
Holidays celebrations, 93–97
Honey, 68, 70–71, 82–83; Butter, Apple, 310; Chicken, Honey Baked, 234; Cookies, Nut Raisin, 253; Cornish Hens, Honey Baked, 235; Dressing, Apple, 184; Dressing, Pineapple, 186; Frosting, Butter, 285; Salad, Banana, 164

I

Icing. *See* Frosting and icing
Illness, diet during, 96–97

J

Jamaican Baked Bananas, 264
Jams. *See* Spreads and jams
Juices, 68

K

Kabobs, Orange Vegetable, 220–21
Kamut, 74
Ketchup, 66, 304
Kiwifruit Spritzer, 120

L

Lamb Pilaf, 236
Lemon(s): Lemonade, 121; Soup, Greek, 197
Liquid diet, 96–97

M

Maintenance diet, 22
Mandarin Almond Salad, 170
Maple sugar, 68, 71, 83; Frosting, 285
Maple syrup, 68, 71, 83; Apple Sweet Potato Bake, 217; Butter Spread, 312; Carrots, 218; Hasty Pudding, 295
Margarine, 65
Mayonnaise, 69; Eggless, 305; Ginger, 168; Mock, 185
Meat: allowed foods, 59; shopping for, 69; *See also* specific meat
Meat loaf: Chicken or Turkey, 230; Quick Savory, 239
Medic-Alert bracelets, 23
Melon(s): Cantaloupe Sherbet, 261; Chicken Salad with Fresh Fruit, 167; Shake, Fresh, 117; Watermelon Sherbet, 267
Menus: planning, 32, 100; sample, 102–7; terms for shellfish, 51–52
Milk: -containing foods, 44–46; FALCPA and, 16; -free cooking, 81; living without, 111; outgrowing allergies, 23; substitutions for, 69
Minestrone, 198
Mock Mayonnaise, 185

Mollusks, 52; *See also* Shellfish and seafood
MSG, 64
Muffins, 124; Banana Oat, 139; Blueberry Oat, 136; Corn, 137; Nut Butter Rice, 138; Oat, 139; Raisin, 139; Rice Flour, 140
Mushroom(s): Kabobs, Orange Vegetable, 220–21; Pilaf, Barley and, 206; Sauce, 231; Stuffed, 210

N

Navy Bean Soup, 199
New ingredients worksheet, 32–33
Nut(s): allowed foods, 60; Bread, Zucchini, 132; Cookies, Honey Raisin, 253; Cookies, Raisin, 257; freezing, 101; meal, 74; *See also* Almond(s); Pecan(s)
Nut butter(s), 69, 313; Bars, Chocolate Crunch, 252; Bars, Granola, 255; Frosty Freezer Treats, 101, 262; Muffins, Rice, 138
Nut milk, 69; Cream, Whipped, 306

O

Oat flour, 73; Bread, 130; Bread, Carrot, 129; Cake, Banana, 275; Cake, Oatmeal-Raisin Carrot, 279–80; Coffee Cake, Streusel-Topped, 131; Cookies, Banana Oatmeal, 247; Cookies, Butterscotch, 251; Cookies, Maple Oatmeal, 254; Crackers, Oatmeal, 145; Muffins, Oat, 139;

Noodles, 303; Pancake or Waffle Batter, 155; Pie Shell, 286

Oatmeal: Apple, 151; Apple Spice, 152; Bars, Nut Butter Granola, 255; Bread, 130; Cake, -Raisin Carrot, 279–80; Candy, Carob, 269; Cookies, Banana, 247; Cookies, Maple, 254; Crisp, Apple, 258; Crisp, Quick Banana, 271; Granola, Apple Nutmeg, 147, 150; Granola, Crunchy, 153; Muffins, Banana, 139; Muffins, Blueberry, 136; Oatcakes, Scottish, 144; Rice Brown Betty, 297; Stuffing, 219

Oils and fats, 60, 65, 70

Onion, 16, 17

Orange(s): Chicken Salad, Hawaiian, 169; Chicken Salad with Fresh Fruit, 167; Duck, Cherry and, 228; Kabobs, Vegetable, 220–21; Salad, Avocado Almond, 162–63; Salad, Mandarin Almond, 170; Salad, Rice, 172

P

Pancakes: Batter, 155; Dutch Potato, 154; Potato, 156

Paper goods, 70

Pasta and noodles: allowed foods, 57; Oat, 303; Rice Sticks, China Bowl, 208; substitutions for, 75, 78

Peach(es): Drink, Banana-, 114; Granola, Amaranth, 149; Pie, with Almond Crust, 288

Peanut(s): biological classifications of, 48; -containing foods, 53–54; FALCPA and, 16; permanent allergy to, 23

Pears, Baked, 260

Pea Soup, 200

Pecan(s): Balls, 256; Cookies, Honey Raisin, 253; Pie, Pumpkin, 289

Pepper, 16, 17

Pie(s), 272; Chocolate, Old-Fashioned, 287; Peach, with Almond Crust, 288; Pumpkin Pecan, 289; Strawberry, 291

Pie shells and crusts: Oatmeal, 286; Rice or Rye, 290

Pilaf: Barley and Mushroom, 206; Lamb, 236; Rice, 222

Pineapple: Cake, Tapioca, 282; Chicken Salad, Hawaiian, 169; Chicken Salad with Fresh Fruit, 167; Cooler, Banana-, 113; Dressing, Honey, 186; Kabobs, Orange Vegetable, 220–21; Porcupines, 265; Pork Chops with Rice, 237; Slush, 118

Pork, 18; Pineapple Chops with Rice, 237; Pork Chop Spanish Rice, 238

Potato(es): Hash Brown, 216; Pancakes, 156; Pancakes, Dutch, 154; Salad, 174; Soup, Chicken and, 191; Soup, Creamy, 196; Soup, Vegetable Beef, 202; Stew, Beef and Vegetable, 189

Potato chips, 70

Potato flour/starch, 63, 74–75; Almond Crescents, 245; Cake, Fruity Spice, 278; Cookies, Applesauce, 246; Cookies, Raisin Nut, 257

Poultry: allowed foods, 59; Cornish Hens, Honey Baked, 235; Duck, Cherry and Orange, 228; shopping for, 69; Turkey Loaf, 230; See also Chicken

Prawns, 52

Pudding(s): Apple Tapioca, 292; Apple Tapioca Supreme, 293; Hasty, 295; Rice, 147, 298; Rice, Fruity, 294; Rice Brown Betty, 297; Vanilla, 296

Pumpernickel Bread, 133–34

Pumpkin Pecan Pie, 289

Q

Quinoa, 76

R

Raisin(s): Cake, Oatmeal- Carrot, 279–80; Cake, Spice, 281; Coconut-Covered, 270; Cookies, Honey Nut, 253; Cookies, Nut, 257; Muffins, 139

Recipes: development of, 34–35, 72–73; organizing, 36

Relish, Cranberry, 223

Rennet, 46

Restaurants, shellfish and, 51–52

Rice: Apple Rice Betty, 259; Chicken with Tomato Rice Stuffing, Baked, 226; Confetti, 209; Pilaf, 222; Pilaf, Lamb, 236; Pork Chops, Pineapple, 237; Pork Chop Spanish Rice, 238; Pudding, 147, 298; Pudding, Fruity, 294; Salad, Orange, 172; Soup, Greek Lemon, 197

Rice cakes, 70

Rice flour, 73–74; Biscuits,

143; Biscuits, Almond, 141; Bread, 134–35; Brownies, 250; Cake, Chiffon "Pound", 277; Cake, Spice, 281; Cookies, Blueberry Delight, 250; Cookies, Raisin Nut, 257; Muffins, 140; Muffins, Corn, 137; Muffins, Nut Butter Rice, 138; Pecan Balls, 256; Pie Crust, 290; Rice Brown Betty, 297; Waffles, 157

Rice milk, 69

Rice Sticks, China Bowl, 208

Rice syrup, 71

Rye flour, 73, 74; Pie Crust, 290; Pumpernickel Bread, 133–34; Rye Crisps, 146

S

Salad(s), 158; Apple Gelatin, 161; Avocado Almond Orange, 162–63; Avocado Stuffed with Tuna, 163; Banana Honey, 164; Chicken, Hawaiian, 169; Chicken, with Fresh Fruit, 167; Chicken, with Ginger Mayonnaise, 168; Chicken Grape, 165; Chicken Rice, with Cashews, 166; Coleslaw, 173; Fruit, Sunny, 177; Fruit Gelatin, Molded, 171; Mandarin Almond, 170; Orange Rice, 172; Potato, 174; Salmon, 175; Sunflower, 176; Tuna, 178; Tuna, Luau, 179; Wild Rice, 181; Wild Rice Chicken, 180

Salad dressing(s): Basic, with Herbs, 182; Celery Seed, 183; Citrus, 162–63; French, 158, 184; Honey Apple, 184; Mock Mayonnaise, 185; Pineapple

Honey, 186

Salmon Salad, 175

Salt, 70

Sandwiches: Sloppy Joes, 240

Sauce(s), 299; allowed foods, 59; Catsup, 66, 304; Mayonnaise, Eggless, 305; Mushroom, 231; spaghetti, 100–101; Tartar, 308; Tomato, Quick, 307; White, 309

Scones. See Biscuits and scones

Scottish Oatcakes, 144

Sea salt, 70

Seasonings and spices, 16, 17, 18, 61, 70

Seed(s), 60, 69

Shellfish and seafood: allergy to, 23, 50–52; biological classifications, 327; FALCPA and, 16; restaurants and, 51–52

Sherbet: Cantaloupe, 261; Fruit, 263; Watermelon, 267

Shrimp, 50, 52

Sloppy Joes, 240

Slow cooker cooking, 101, 108–10, 187

Soft diet, 96–97

Soup(s) and stew(s), 187; Beef and Vegetable, 189; Beef Stock, 190; Chicken, 192; Chicken and Potato, 191; Chicken Broth, 193; Corn Chowder, 194; Lemon, Greek, 197; Minestrone, 198; Navy Bean, 199; Pea, 200; Potato, Creamy, 196; Tomato, 201; Vegetable, Cream of, 195; Vegetable Beef, 202

Soybean(s): -containing foods, 46–48; FALCPA and, 16; outgrowing allergies, 23; peanut allergies and, 53

Spelt, 74; Scones, Dried Cherry Spelt, 142–43

Spinach: Flounder Florentine, 233

Spreads and jams, 299; Apple Honey Butter, 310; Blueberry, 311; Maple Butter, 312; Nut Butter, 69, 313; Strawberry, 314

Squash: Kabobs, Orange Vegetable, 220–21; See also Zucchini

Staples and condiments, 299; allowed foods, 59; Catsup, 66, 304; Corn-Free Baking Powder, 301; Cottage Cheese, 302; Cream, Whipped, 306; Mayonnaise, Eggless, 305; Oat Noodles, 303

Stock/broth, 64, 190, 193

Strawberry(ies): Chicken Salad with Fresh Fruit, 167; freezing, 118; Jam, 314; Muffins, Rice Flour, 140; Pie, 291; Sherbet, 263; Slush, 118

Streusel-Topped Coffee Cake, 131

Stuffed Mushrooms, 210

Substitutions, 32, 72–73; for chocolate, 65; for cornstarch, 62–63; for milk, 69; for pasta and noodles, 75, 78; for wheat, 62–63, 65, 67, 73–78

Sugar-free cooking, 82–83

Sunflower Salad, 176

Sweeteners, 61, 66, 68, 70–71, 82–83

Sweet potato(es) and yams: Casserole, Baked, 205, Dutch Yam Supreme, 212; Maple Apple Bake, 217

T

Tapioca, 280; Apple, 292, 293

Tapioca flour, 75; Cake, Pineapple, 282

Tartar Sauce, 308

Tea, 16, 17

Thickeners, 57, 62–63, 74–75, 79

Timesaving techniques, 99–101

Tomato(es): Catsup, 66, 304; Chicken with Tomato Rice Stuffing, Baked, 226; Eggplant with, 214; Oriental Skillet, 221; Pork Chop Spanish Rice, 238; Sauce, Quick, 307; Sloppy Joes, 240; Soup, 201

Tomato Juice Cocktail, 122

Trader Joe's, 46

Tree nuts: allergy to, 23, 50; -containing foods, 48–49; FALCPA and, 16; meal, 74; shopping for, 71; See also Almond(s); Nut(s); Pecan(s)

Tropical Shake, 123

Tuna: Avocado Stuffed with, 163; Salad, 178; Salad Luau, 179

Turkey Loaf, 230

V

Vanilla, 71; Pudding, 296

Vegetable(s), 203; allowed foods, 58–59; biological classifications, 322–28; Kabobs, Orange, 220–21; shopping for, 71; Soup, Beef, 202; Soup, Cream of, 195; starchy, as thickener, 75; Stew, Beef and, 189; See also specific vegetables

W

Waffles: Batter, 155; Rice, 157

Water chestnuts, 48

Watermelon Sherbet, 267

Wheat: -containing foods, 40; FALCPA and, 16; -free cooking, 73–79; outgrowing allergies, 23; substitutions for, 62–63, 65, 67, 73–78

Whey, 44, 45

White Sauce, 309

Wild rice: Chicken Salad, 180; Salad, 181

X

Xanthan gum, 71, 79, 135

Y

Yams. See Sweet potato(es) and yams

Yeast, 18

Z

Zucchini: Nut Bread, 132; Oriental Tomato Skillet, 66